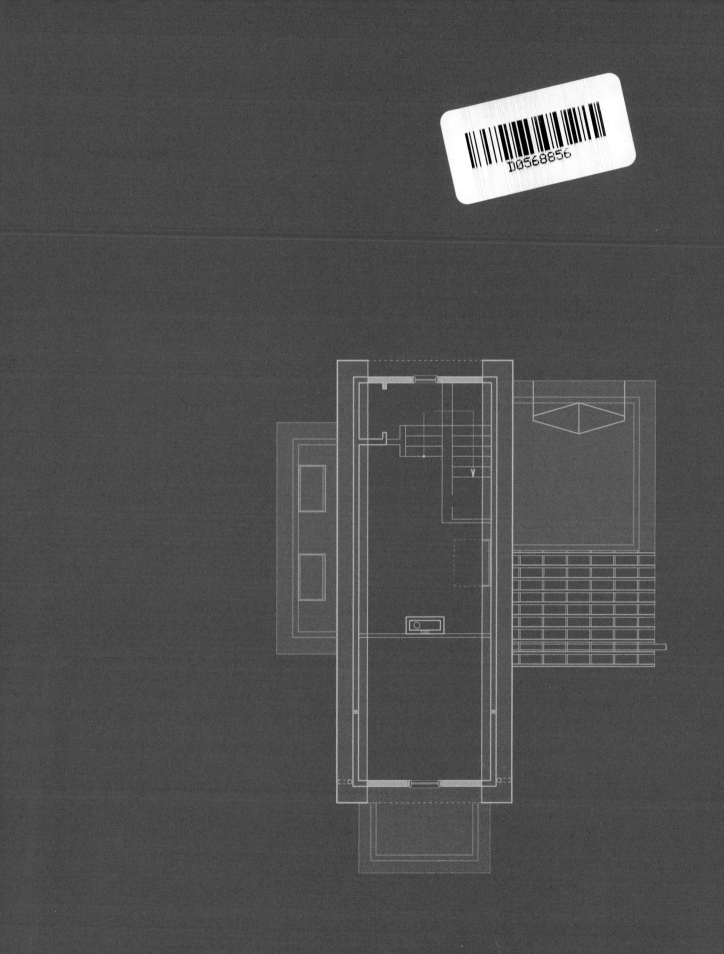

WELCOMING HOME

WELCOMING HOME

Michaela Mahady

GIBBS SMITH
TO ENRICH AND INSPIRE HUMANKIND

First Edition
14 13 12 11 10   5 4 3 2 1

Published by
Gibbs Smith
P.O. Box 667
Layton, Utah 84041

1.800.835.4993 orders
www.gibbs-smith.com

Designed by Debra McQuiston
Printed and bound in China
Gibbs Smith books are printed on either recycled, 100% post-consumer
waste, FSC-certified papers or on paper produced from a 100% certified
sustainable forest/controlled wood source.

Library of Congress Cataloging-in-Publication Data

Mahady, Michaela.
  Welcoming home / Michaela Mahady. — 1st ed.
    p. cm.
  ISBN-13: 978-1-4236-0321-4
  ISBN-10: 1-4236-0321-4
  1. Architecture, Domestic—Psychological aspects. I. Title.
  NA7125.M333 2010
  728.01—dc22
                    2010011371

For Theresia Kershbaumer Mayrhofer, my grandmother,
Waltrude Mayrhofer Mahady, my mother, and Yana Theresa Pietras, my
daughter, who have taught me much about living and loving in houses.

CONTENTS

PREFACE

꙰ HOW IS IT THAT SOME HOUSES SEEM TO SPEAK to us and remain lodged in our memory? What qualities do such dwellings possess?

The answers to these questions are different for each individual. Yet there are identifiable characteristics that make a house feel "just right," qualities that we innately understand. Some houses can appear aloof, even unapproachable. But others reach out to us; they can seem like wise, comforting friends. They seem to say, "Welcome, come on in. You will be comfortable, warm, safe, and secure here."

The most satisfying home has a personality. It projects a sense of shelter, protection, and permanence, as well as a promise of comfort, delight, maybe even happy magic, within its walls.

The places that call out to us are places that draw us in through our senses and emotions. They are the places where we can most truly be ourselves. Identifying the characteristics of such places is an essential aspect of designing and creating a home.

INTRODUCTION

ARCHITECTS, INCLUDING MYSELF, are trained to analyze situations, and from that analysis, to categorize and identify potential principles of design. We seek to find universality in elements of design, hoping to discover an ideal design system. It's kind of like a search for the Holy Design Grail or the Holy Cookbook of Design, expecting that there is a foolproof way to mix up some ingredients and end up with a good result: a good house or building or community. We use the principles we identify to further the design of our own work, according to our own personal ideals and values. We may foster and promote the notion that these principles should guide all acts of building.

Those architects who aspire to write books about design either fall into the trap of systematizing their own personal ideas as universally applicable truth, by writing a New Holy Cookbook of Design. Or they fall into a quicksand of hubris, by illustrating those ideas with their own work (surprise!). So I proceed, with one foot set firmly in either trap.

When we want to learn how to cook, we do use cookbooks. There are many excellent "design cookbooks" to guide us; my favorites are listed throughout these pages. This book, though, is not intended to be a design cookbook. It is rather perhaps a search for the Inner Design Cook in all of us. While I certainly do not think that my perceptions or design solutions are right for everyone, I do believe that an examination of how we as individuals perceive and respond to space, form, and environment is a worthy endeavor. Those perceptions lie in each individual, waiting to be discovered.

Because of our training in systems and logic, we architects rely on our rational, intellectual faculties to create buildings. Regrettably, we receive less training in understanding the full range of ways that human beings experience space and built form. It is especially difficult to quantify and codify the areas of human experience that relate to our senses, our emotional responses to buildings, and the feelings engendered by our experiences in buildings. Although we at least subliminally understand the significance of these issues, we tend to proceed with the design of buildings in a manner that emphasizes intellect over feeling.

The dominance of intellectual understanding over experiential and emotional understanding leads to intellectualized expression: buildings that present clever or innovative ideas, while sometimes offering the human inhabitant little in terms of comfort, serenity, or delight. Senses, feelings, and emotional responses, whether within a building or about a building, are thought of as somehow second rate, involving a lower level of perception. Buildings that are comfortable are dismissed as merely feeling good. Buildings that connect with the emotions are thought of as sentimental.

We are given our bodies, minds, and spirits as tools with which to understand our environment and our lives. We need to find a manner of building that addresses all of these parts of our being. Much of the architecture of the last hundred years has honored intellect and innovation over bodily sensation and experience. Too often, architecturally designed homes celebrate a narrow set of ideas, the splendor of materials and the status or affluence of the homeowner. On the other hand, homes that are not influenced by architects at all tend to be assemblages of the latest trends and amenities supposedly sought by the public. They are rambling concoctions of vacuous spaces, covered over by huge empty roofs, intending to impress by their size and glamorous gadgetry.

These buildings seem to have lost the connection to our human selves and bodies. Yet we crave this connection and find something sorely missing in buildings that lack it. We need to rediscover and understand the links between our bodies and buildings. We can then use those discoveries in the design of our homes.

This volume is a study of how houses speak to us, what messages they send, and how we can come to better understand what they are saying. We will examine how human beings experience space and built form, with an eye to understanding the spatial experiences that form our own preferred personal patterns.

We can use these lessons to create homes that are more responsive to *all* our needs for shelter—physical, psychological, and spiritual. And we can become more aware of our roles in caring for the earth, as we build and dwell on it.

THE PERSONA OF A HOUSE

FROM OUR EARLIEST DAYS, human beings respond to stimuli and environments that nurture our beings. We are drawn to light, voices and sounds, the warmth and safety of our parents' faces and bodies. We are able to sense the difference between peaceful environments, stimulating ones, and those that are harsh or even dangerous. The notion of being "at home" is a re-creation of those early learned responses, in physical form. We create our homes as comforting, safe nests around ourselves, as protection from the outside world, both natural and manmade. Our homes offer us, in the most elemental sense, the security and acceptance of a loving embrace.

A child's first drawings of a house offer many clues about our initial responses to the environment. Those responses reveal the origins of our concepts of house and home. Houses drawn by children often embody human, anthropomorphic characteristics. The body of the house form is sensed as similar to the body of a human being, with a front and a back, a top above and a bottom below. The front of the house is analogous to a face, balanced and orderly. Symmetrically placed windows peer out as eyes, and a central door opens as a mouth. The house's body/face form is often crowned by a pointy hat—a gabled roof that sheds the elements to either side. As children, we borrow the sense of our own bodies and appendages and re-create them as houses with bodylike forms.

This early elemental sensory understanding continues to influence us throughout our lives. We tend to respond strongly to buildings that suggest in some manner a relationship to the symmetrical form of the human body, particularly those in which we can decipher the features of a face.

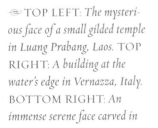

TOP LEFT: *The mysterious face of a small gilded temple in Luang Prabang, Laos.* TOP RIGHT: *A building at the water's edge in Vernazza, Italy.* BOTTOM RIGHT: *An immense serene face carved in stone, at the Bayon temple ruins in Cambodia. A hollowed out interior space exists within it.* BOTTOM LEFT: *The quizzical face on this storefront in Vienna is even more apparent if you turn it upside down.*

We tend to RESPOND STRONGLY
to buildings that suggest
a relationship to the human body,
particularly those in which we decipher
the FEATURES OF A FACE.

Children in a "box house."

The protective shell wrapped around a snail is the most basic and integral form of shelter. Given a large box, a child delights in creating a diminutive house immediately around his body. A child understands the shelter and protection of a house in a similar, very immediate fashion. It is a direct extension of the form of the body, like a warm overcoat that retains the shape of its owner.

Anthropomorphism is defined as ascribing human form or attributes to nonhuman beings or objects. In a similar fashion to architecture that shows structural parallels to the human body, many objects that we use daily exhibit the characteristics of human form. Anthropomorphism is used in advertising, product and toy design, engineering, robotics, storytelling, cartoons, art, and architecture. The projection of human form and values onto objects in our surroundings allows us a sense of familiarity and identification with the world around us. If we feel a positive emotional response to a humanlike object, whether it be a car, a house, a pot, or a tool, we are more likely to engage with the object, use it, and feel "at one" with it.

Recent research has shown that we think and understand not only with the brains in our heads, but also with the hearts and the guts in our torsos. We possess within our bodies an innate kind of knowing and emotional understanding of the spaces around us. We sense this knowledge with our bodies, and we can feel it as a sensation throughout our bodies.

The nervous tissue associated with thought and knowledge is present not only in our brains but also in our hearts and digestive tracts, so that knowing is not exclusively an activity of the brain and intellect, but of the heart and body as well. Thus occurs the real sense of physical pain we experience as a result of profound loss or depression—what we call a broken heart. Or, sometimes we can be at a loss for words as to how we know something or have come to a decision, but if pressed, we will simply say, "I feel it in my gut." The emotional system is closely linked with behavior. The sensation of queasy unease in your stomach is not a product of the imagination. Rather, it demonstrates that emotions affect muscular systems and digestive systems, clueing the body to react in a specific way to a situation. Things

that smell and taste good cause the body to inhale, salivate, and digest. Bad smells or tastes make the mouth as well as the stomach muscles contract involuntarily to eject the contents. Feelings and emotions play a key role in helping us decipher good from bad, or danger from safety.[1]

Donald A. Norman is a cognitive scientist and cofounder of a consulting firm that aids companies in the design of human-oriented products. In the 1980s, he wrote a book called *The Design of Everyday Things.* He observed recently that while writing it, "I didn't take emotion into account. I addressed utility, function, and form, all in a logical, dispassionate way—even though I'm infuriated by poorly designed objects." He followed it by another book in 2004 titled *Emotional Design: Why We Love (or Hate) Everyday Things.* In it, he describes his change of direction: "New scientific advances in our understanding of the brain [show] how emotion and cognition are thoroughly intertwined. We now understand how important emotion is to everyday life, how valuable. Sure, utility and usability are important, but without fun and pleasure, joy and excitement, and yes, anxiety and anger, fear and rage, our lives would be incomplete."

Norman goes on to describe three levels of perception: the visceral, the behavioral, and the reflective, all of which interact to guide how we deal with the situations presented by daily life. The visceral level does not reason; instead it works by "pattern matching." Positive visceral responses react to exposure to:

❖ Warm, comfortably lit places
❖ Temperate climates
❖ Sweet tastes and smells
❖ Bright colors
❖ "Soothing" sounds, simple melodies and rhythms
❖ Harmonious music and sounds
❖ Caresses
❖ Smiling faces
❖ Rhythmic beats
❖ "Attractive" people
❖ Symmetrical objects
❖ Rounded, smooth objects

Negative visceral responses occur when we are exposed to the following:

❖ Heights
❖ Sudden, unexpected loud sounds or bright lights
❖ "Looming" objects that seem to be about to hit the observer
❖ Extreme hot or cold
❖ Darkness

---

1. *Ways of Knowing, Exploring Intuition's Role in Health & Healing.* University of Minnesota Center for Spirituality and Healing and the Life Science Foundation.

- ❖ Empty flat places, like deserts
- ❖ Crowded dense terrain
- ❖ Crowds of people
- ❖ Rotting smells, bitter tastes
- ❖ Sharp objects
- ❖ Harsh, abrupt, grating, or discordant sounds
- ❖ Misshapen human bodies
- ❖ Snakes and spiders

Our most basic reactions to our environment are visceral. Our bodies tell us, before the influence of logic and reason, which environments are safe, nurturing, and comforting. They tell us how things feel. And what we think is inevitably affected by what we feel. Our recurrent experiences lead to adjustments in our behavior; they form our thought patterns, attitudes, and personality traits.

The association of house form with human faces and bodies is understood at a visceral, emotional level, and can be thought of as an archetypal pattern or idea. This body-oriented understanding is communicated not only by the façade, or "face" of the home, but by the inside of the home as well. The central connective tissue of the home consists of relationships between the main places in which we interact with others and conduct everyday activities. One often hears the expression that the hearth, or the kitchen, is the heart of the house. This was very much the case historically in the farmhouse, where the kitchen and its woodstove were seen as a central mechanism, a "heart" connected to all the daily activities of the family's life. The ritual of providing daily sustenance to the family formed the hierarchy of connective relationships between the rooms. Daily tasks, preparation of food, eating together, spending time together at the end of the workday, and nurturing children all took place in the same space, or in closely connected ones. The warmth of the hearth used for food preparation in early American homes, or of a massive iron cookstove, or a stove clad with ceramic tiles fueled with wood, drew the inhabitants of the house around it to share its resonating heat, to gather and share stories and news of the day.

Sleeping quarters were often above, located in the space beneath the roof, the protective "hat" of the house. The "bowels" of the house, the basement or cellar, received the protection and the temperate nature of the earth around them and were used for storage of foodstuffs and water. The attic, perched within the very peak of the roof, closest to the sky, can be thought of as the "mind" of the house. The attic of a house is akin to a lofty, cerebral center, a repository of stored memories, and a place to escape to for the expression of new creative ideas. These notions are evident in spaces like an artist's loft, a writer's attic garret, or the ivory tower of an intellectual who prefers to live with his or her head in the clouds.

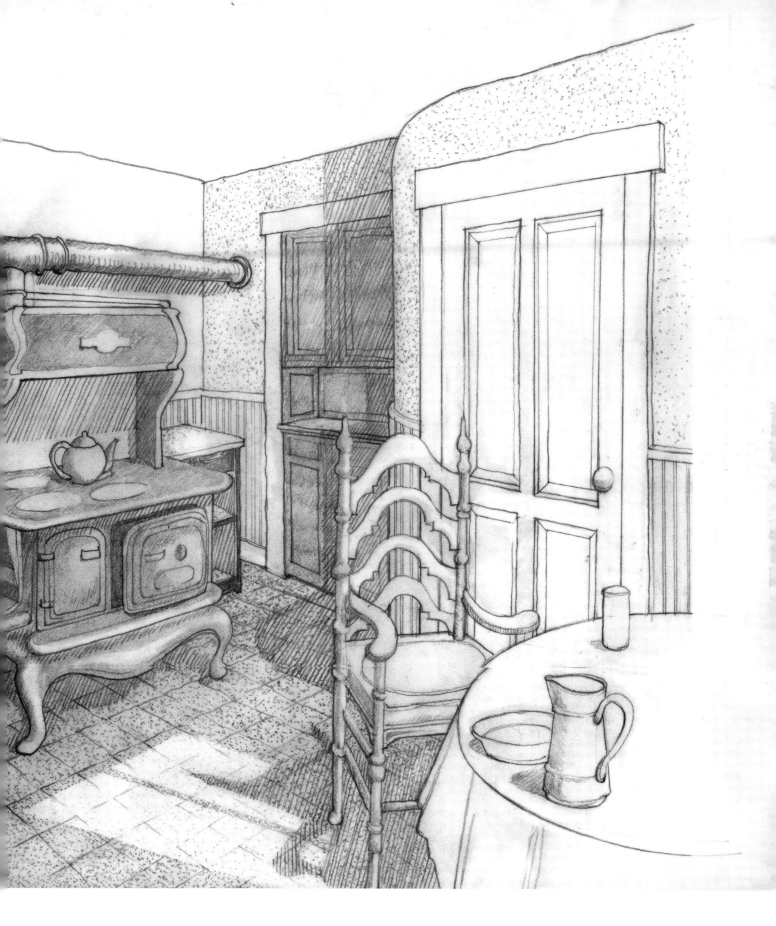

These eminently understandable characteristics of houses have been used and re-used, both unconsciously and purposefully, since man began to make shelter for himself.

They have been expressed literally and interpreted abstractly. The simple, ordered form of such a house lent itself well to a logical and pragmatic method of construction, whether it was of mud, straw, bricks, or lumber. Such houses abound throughout the world, with variously shaped roof/hats, depending on the nature of the climatic elements from which the inhabitants needed protection.

We understand these sheltering, protective houses in an emotional and visceral manner. We experience them in an elemental sense: they contain only what is most necessary for our physical, emotional, and spiritual health, as individuals and family units. Because they consist only of what is necessary, they consume less land, materials, and energy during their lifespans, tending often to be smaller and more compact than their more voracious neighbors. And, they possess a palpable emotional draw on our psyches. They *speak* to us, offering us the promise of safety, peace, and serenity within their walls.

> "If a building makes us light up,
> it is not because we see order; any row of file cabinets
> is ordered. What we recognize and love is
> the same kind of pattern we see in every face, the
> pattern of our own life form."
>
> —Jonathan Hale, from *The Old Way of Seeing*

A HOUSE THAT SAYS HELLO

EARLY IN MY CAREER AS AN ARCHITECT, I designed a house for a heavily wooded piece of land near a large lake in Minnesota. The house was to be built speculatively by Kyle and Laurie Hunt of Kyle Hunt and Partners Construction Company. It was also to be featured on the semi-annual Parade of Homes in the Twin City area and on the television series "Hometime." We named the house Maple Forest after the dense woodland of maple trees that populated its site. We located the house among the trees, overlooking the woods from a small swell of land that rose in the middle of the site.

I have learned many lessons from the Maple Forest House. At the time it was perhaps the third or fourth house that I had designed and seen all the way through construction, with architect Wayne Branum and Christine Johnson. Watching it grow, under the hands of the talented, skillful (and extremely patient!) craftsmen who brought it into existence, was a continuing delight and an unforgettable experience. Every time I drove down the winding lane approaching the house, I eagerly peered through the tall trunks of the maple tree to glimpse again the big front gabled form. I began to realize that there was something very special about the house. Every time I arrived, it seemed almost to speak to me, or to my heart. I felt, or imagined, that the house almost smiled; it was glad to see me, again and again (after all, who else would have so painstakingly pored over every inch of its maple and cherry trim?). The house greeted me and pulled me into it. Every time I arrived, I felt the house saying hello. And after a time, I found myself mentally answering, "Hello, House," as I walked up to it.

FACING: *These interior French doors separate the study from the hall and stairway opposite. The design of the glass echoes the rhythmic lines of the wood screen at the stairwell.*

ABOVE: *A finely detailed built-in bench of maple and cherry wood is located next to the entry. It graciously offers a spot to sit down, take off your boots, and stow your backpack or briefcase in the adjacent cabinet.*

Of course, I did not share these "revelations" with the patient carpenters, who may well have been less happy to see me than the house was. In fact, I did not speak about my emotional attachment to the house to anyone at all. To think of the house as an actual being, one that could greet me and welcome me and reassure me, seemed naïve, childish, potentially wacky. Nevertheless, I kept saying hello, and so did the house. In the end we became quite fond of one another.

After construction, the house was featured on the Parade of Homes in the Twin Cities metropolitan area and was visited by thousands of people. I heard their comments as they toured the home, and I began to receive the first of many phone

calls about the house. I was amazed to learn that many people had the same kind of strong emotional reaction that I had experienced. One woman spoke to me at length, telling me how the house had brought tears of joy to her eyes as she walked up to it, but she didn't know why.

The construction process of the house was shown on the television series "Hometime," and those episodes were repeated numerous times on the Learning Channel of PBS. It was featured in *Fine Homebuilding* magazine and then in *Better Homes and Gardens*, which offered the plan of the house for sale to the public.

It eventually became the most popular plan that *Better Homes and Gardens* had ever featured. Thousands of plans were sold and I received hundreds of phone calls about the house. (I still receive them occasionally now!) The people who called would start off with questions and comments about predictable subjects: the wood, the stain colors, the roofing, the stairs, the stone fireplace, the cabinets. Eventually many of them would work their way around to telling me, sometimes almost shyly, how they felt about the house. They would often say things like, "It seems kind of funny, but I simply can't tell you how much my wife (or husband) and I just *love* this house. We absolutely fell in love with it as soon as we set eyes on it."

"Love at first sight . . ." it seems the house must have been speaking to them too!

Initially, I didn't know how to respond to those comments. But as the conversations continued to happen frequently, I would simply say, "I know what you mean. I feel that way about the house too."

Over the years I have tried to analyze why all those people and I felt that way about Maple Forest. How did that particular house evoke such a strong emotional

ABOVE RIGHT: A corner of comfortable upholstered benches opens to the kitchen space. A special table crafted of bird's-eye maple and cherry wood, designed by architect Wayne Branum, sits in the midst of the corner nook. ABOVE: A deep, low-arched portion of ceiling creates a sheltered feeling around the hearth. FACING: The kitchen space is differentiated from the living area beyond by an arched ceiling that spans between maple and cherry cabinets at either end.

response? I've tried to identify other dwellings that speak to me in the same way, like a very dear, reassuring, welcoming person would. In addition, I've tried to figure out the messages that other buildings send, ones that don't make me feel the same way. This is tricky stuff; I don't at all assume that my response will be the same as anyone else's. And yet I know that a great number of people did respond that way. Is it a personal response only, or a cultural one, or even a universal one?

I never could quite answer that question. I certainly do not think of the elements that speak to me most strongly as universal. And yet, many of them stem from an understanding of built form as similar to human form, which is a deep response that many people experience. For each of us, the most crucial thing is the continual search for the characteristics of and the relationships between the things that feel most right, satisfying, and beloved. These are one's personal "patterns," by which we can decide what to build, what to do, how to spend our lives. Christopher Alexander, in his first volume *The Timeless Way of Building*, describes a similar phenomenon most eloquently as "The Quality Without a Name."

The Maple Forest House shares some common characteristics with other homes that speak to me strongly. Those qualities stem from the way the house form itself suggests a welcoming, protective presence, related to a human face or body:

1. A FRONT FACING GABLE
The slightly projecting gabled front of Maple Forest, with its dominant, oversized hemisphere of glass, seems almost to gently smile. It is one's first visual impression of the house, after which one gradually absorbs the overall form of the cross gable, the winding drive that leads to the entry, and the garage beyond, whose doors are tucked away to the side, almost out of sight. The composition of the façade is not precisely an anthropomorphic face, but somehow, the curved line above the ample window suggests a serene, smiling brow. The gable and its window come out to greet you.

2. A BIG ROOF
The roof that hovers over Maple Forest casts protective wings around the building. It declares that the house is a safe haven, shelter from the elements as well as from the rigorous pace of everyday life. Key to this sense of protection is the presence of deep overhanging eaves, which extend out from the building, stretching over the heads of both inhabitants and visitors. They give a sense of shelter above one's body around the entire perimeter of the house; the body senses the shelter below the eaves as a safe place. As well, they protect the walls of the house from weather, and shade the windows from the heat and glare of the direct summer sun.

The entry to the house is on the front porch, sheltered by a "catslide roof," a curved extension of the major gable.

Not only is the roof large and dominant, but its deep eavelines also extend out close to the ground, just above the height of the main floor windows. This heightens the sense of shelter that they provide. It also reduces the house height in a way that gives the house a more welcoming, less formidable personality than a much taller two- or three-story structure.

To bring the roof down in relation to the house, we framed the second floor with shorter knee walls, from which the main gables arise. The upper floors are thus contained within the space inside the volume of the roof. Their varied ceiling heights follow the rooflines, so that the bedrooms feel the embrace of the sheltering roof around them.

3. A COVERED PORCH.

A curved extension of Maple Forest's dominant roof swoops over to cover an entry porch that extends along the length of the house. The porch floor wraps around the house, spilling over into a large semicircular veranda on a deep stone base. The railings of the porch are fitted with lantern-type lights that are integrated into the posts: the lanterns' inviting glow broadly suggests that the house is a very good place to be, saying, "Why don't you come over and sit down?" The message of the porch is the preface to the welcoming spaces within the house itself.

4. SHELTERED SPACES WITHIN.

My clients often describe to me the enduring allure of older homes. Heaven knows I have long been quite susceptible to that attraction myself. Part of it has to do with the fond memories of time spent within such homes. Also, the homes of the past were built with a careful sense of scale to the human form. The ceilings, as Goldilocks might say, are not too high, not too low, but just right for the activity that occurs within them.

I have been greatly influenced by my memories and experiences living in and learning from older homes. However, in the past, homes were differently zoned. Public and private realms were defined in a manner reflecting the more formal social and familial customs of the day, rather than the less formal way we live now. The rooms were thought of as quite separate and distinct from one another. In particular, the kitchen of an older American home was typically sequestered at the rear of the house and was quite small in scale compared to other rooms in the house. It was considered a functional service area. Meal preparation and daily tasks were either the responsibility of servants or the lady of the house. In neither case were those activities to be observed by others, so the kitchen was purpose-fully separated from the public rooms by walls, corridors, and intermediate pantry spaces. The role of the kitchen within the home has radically changed within the past century, shifting from a place of hidden unacknowledged activity for support players to a starring role. The kitchen is now an extremely visible space, sometimes to the point of being a showy object of display. It is open to almost all of the major public rooms in the house. The structure of the American family changed during that time, from having a single wage earner to two. Resultantly, time with family and friends became more precious; the time spent during food preparation and daily tasks became shared time. The kitchen has become a social space, where family members gather to unwind and relate the experiences of the day, and where we

ABOVE: *A curved eyebrow window in a bedroom dormer is surrounded by a low arched ceiling, with a simple built-in desk just below the window. It is an intimate, sheltered spot for writing, study, or computer use.*
FACING: *Built-in cabinets surround an inviting window seat in the main bedroom. The deep arched ceiling above reduces the height of the room's ceiling, forming a cozy, sheltered spot to sit and enjoy a book or to gaze at the treetops outside.*

entertain our friends while we cook. In homes that are built today, we often see the kitchen space flow into areas for living, dining, and relaxation, and connected to outdoor areas for similar activities, reflecting more casual social customs and our desire to maximize time spent together. Sometimes the old, separate formal living and dining areas of the house persist in the front of the home. The rear of the house then duplicates the functions of those spaces and closely links them to the kitchen. The living and dining areas often remain in the front of the home, offering a buffer between the unexpected visitor and the realm of family and friends. Sometimes these rooms are appointed in such a manner that they are hardly used at all.

The Maple Forest House, as one of the first houses I designed, was greatly influenced by the experiential aspects of older homes. But it was designed to be responsive to the more casual mode of present-day life. The kitchen, breakfast nook, living area, and dining area are all open to one another. Yet, in the manner of older homes, the open space is defined and shaped by varying ceiling heights, surface treatments, and carefully placed architectural elements. Broad arched ceilings frame the kitchen and living areas, culminating at versatile built-in cabinets that serve both spaces. The breakfast area is an L-shaped built-in nook, a "sitzbank" tucked into a cozy corner, inspired by fond memories of time spent at my grandmother's kitchen table. The dominant stone hearth in the living room is visible from all the shared public spaces and is sheltered by a low arched ceiling.

Upstairs, the alcove spaces shaped by the roof dormers create a sense of shelter around the bathtub, and a curved ceiling in the eyebrow dormer of the roof defines a space for a desk. Another deeply arched ceiling skirts the perimeter of the big hemispherical window, lending a feeling of enclosure and shelter to the comfortable window seat below.

The interior of the house contains not only well arranged rooms suitable for family life; it also continues the welcoming message of the house's exterior presence by the many ways in which it offers particular, very special places in it to simply *be*. These places are located at the edges of the rooms, or in between the rooms. The window seats, the arched writing nook in the bedroom, and the cushioned bench in the entry are small-scaled private spaces, offering a place for one person (or two at the most), to be at ease, connected to the activities in the house, but somehow a bit separate from it. They are of small scale, to closely surround the body of a person, echoing perhaps the sense of enclosure and protection one might have felt as a child playing under a table draped with a long tablecloth. They are like little houses within the safe haven of the house itself.

Perhaps the aspect of Maple Forest that most recalls an earlier era of homebuilding is its interior millwork. Window frames and doors are traced with a two-piece composite trim: $3^1/2''$-wide maple boards capped with narrow cherry backband. The trim doesn't stop at the openings, though, as it might have in an older home. Instead, it continues on, delineating the edges of the lowered ceilings between rooms and

A spacious bathroom adjoins the main bedroom. Alcoves create separate, private areas within it for the tub and water closet.

creating a continuous band of wood trim around the room at the height of the tops of the doors. (I absorbed this technique from the work of our former partner, Sarah Susanka, who at the time was dubbed "Our Lady of Perpetual Trim.") This continuous banding defines each individual space within the whole, creating a delicate sense of enclosure around each one. In addition, it laces the spaces together, creating a pleasing and orderly whole. The eye immediately understands this, sensing continuity and coherence between the rooms and spaces, a clarity of how the pieces relate to the whole. The rooms are individually delineated, yet bound together visually.

5. DETAIL AND ORNAMENT.

The Maple Forest House abounds with expressive detail and ornament. The curved brackets that support the roof of the porch, the gabled peaks of the roof, and the cantilevered second floor are oversized for their structural job. But the exaggeration of their size and scale bespeaks a sense of sturdy substance and strength. These brackets are of thick heavy timbers, 8 × 8 and 8 × 10 pieces of cedar. They seem highly reliable, more than capable of holding the big roof overhead securely in place. Similarly, the front door is extra wide and thick; it is satisfyingly heavy and massive when it is swung open or closed. These details reinforce the notion that the house is a strong, protective presence.

The gracious curves of the brackets are witness to the fact that someone worked a long time to shape and smooth them. The mark of the human hand is readily apparent there, and it resonates through the house, in the curved detailing of the tops of windows, the ceilings, the staircase, the welcoming entry bench, and the expressive motifs of the kitchen table. The glass doors of the study reflect the flowing lines of the staircase across the hall. They are crafted of leaded handblown and beveled glass.

These details invite the touch; when we interpret our environment through the sense of touch, we gain a tactile sense of the places we inhabit. We can also sense the human history of how the building was made. We know that our beloved buildings of the present were made by human hands in the past. I sense this in my own house, which was built in 1920, whenever I run my fingers along the curved surfaces of its fine millwork and cabinetry. We remember, and honor, the skilled people who brought these forms into existence. A house that is built by hand is imbued with the spirit of those who built it; they live on through the beauty and usefulness of the things that they have made for us.

John Ruskin described this well in "The Seven Lamps of Architecture" in 1849. He wrote, "When we build, let us think that we build forever. Let it not be for present delight nor for present use alone. Let it be such work as our descendants will thank us for; and let us think, as we lay stone on stone, that a time is to come when those stones will be held sacred because our hands have touched them, and that men will say, as they look upon the labor and wrought substance of them, 'See! This our father did for us.'"

Substantial brackets of solid cedar timbers support the cantilevered second floor above them.

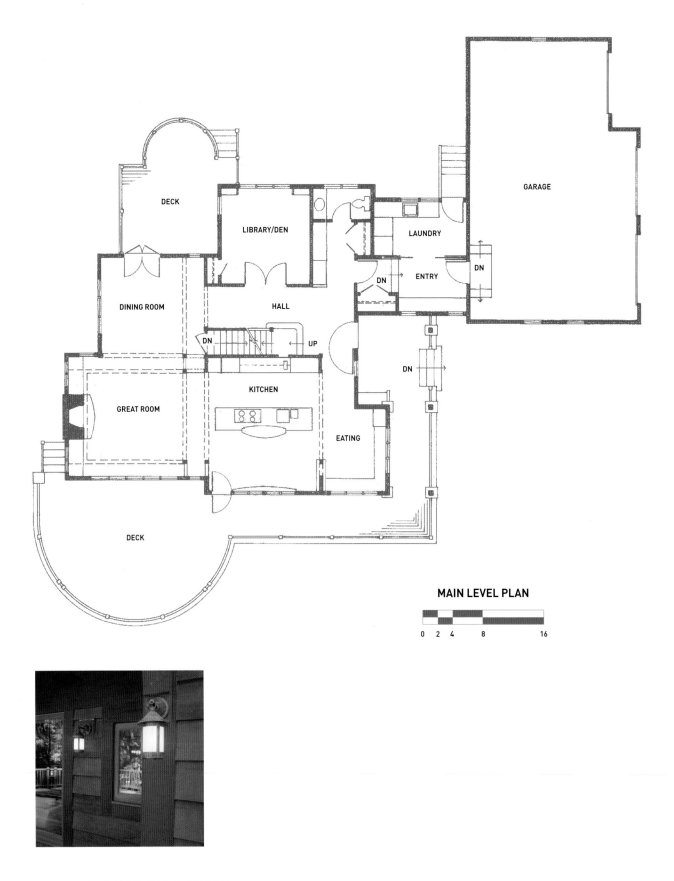

GARAGE

DECK

LIBRARY/DEN

LAUNDRY

DINING ROOM

HALL

DN

ENTRY

DN

DN

UP

DN

GREAT ROOM

KITCHEN

EATING

DECK

MAIN LEVEL PLAN

0 2 4   8   16

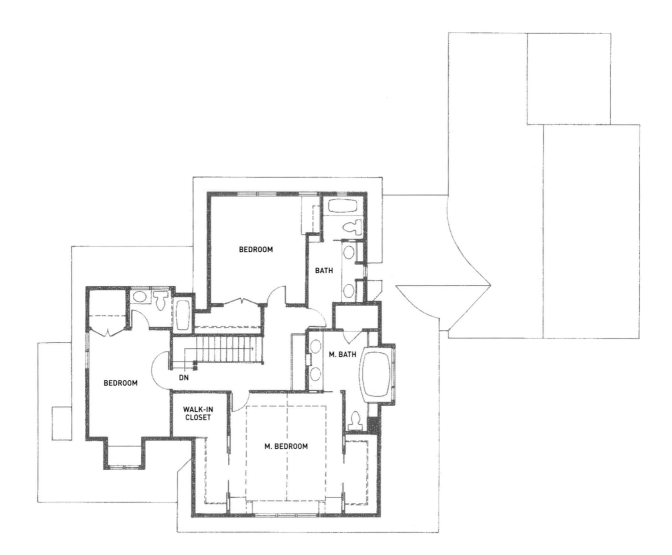

BEDROOM

BATH

BEDROOM

DN

WALK-IN
CLOSET

M. BATH

M. BEDROOM

UPPER LEVEL PLAN

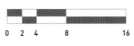

0 2 4   8   16

A HOME
WITH OPEN
ARMS

A KEY COMPONENT OF HOW A HOUSE SPEAKS to us is the manner in which it offers itself as shelter, the way it tells people to enter. The entry and the path to it are one's first experience of the house. As when we meet another person, that first impression is lasting. As we get to know an individual, or a house, better, the relationship deepens. Coming home every day to a welcoming, nurturing home can be a treasured part of one's daily existence. The house, the path to it, and the entry tell you that you are once again protected and safe. You are free to shed the demands and challenges of the outside world, to restore your energy and spirit, and to truly be yourself. To you, the house says, "Welcome home." To a guest, a neighbor, or a passerby, it says hello in a friendly, engaging manner.

In the simplest homes and cottages, the functions of everyday living occurred in one room. Everyone entered at one door, so everyone's experience upon entry was similar. As houses became slightly larger, various living functions began to be separated into rooms. In the New England Cape Cod house, for example, the more formal parlor evolved at the front of the home, the more public side, and was entered through the front door. The buttery, or summer kitchen, the heart of the family's daily work and life, found its place at the rear, more private side of the home. The front door was a celebrated, symbolic entry for the public, prominently and often centrally positioned, flanked with wider trim boards or demi-columns to emphasize its importance. The back door was far more utilitarian and informal in nature, often opening into a shed-like lean-to storage room filled with implements of daily use.

A stone path leads from the detached garage to the family entry of this lake home in Wisconsin. The front entry, shown on the previous page, is symmetrical and ordered, with columns flanking either side of the entry porch under a curved, shell-shaped roof. The family entry is more casual and much less prominent, tucked into an angled link between the main house and a "screen house" porch that echoes the gabled roof forms of the house.

Gradually, these messages of formal front and informal back became codified. As communities grew along rudimentary lanes and streets, commons or squares, both the houses and public buildings "faced front" along them, beginning a long-standing pattern of scale, form, and meaning that persists to this day. The front of the home greeted the public and conveyed the social standing of the family. It tended to be an ordered composition of elements: walkway, stoop, windows, roof and dormer forms, and purposefully placed, manicured plantings. Some homes offered a bit of shelter from the elements at the front door, perhaps a small shed roof supported by decorative brackets, a place to gain temporary protection before entering the parlor or living area also located at the front of the home. This simple shelter grew into a front porch, where a few rocking chairs might offer to passersby a glimpse of the life within the house. It also gave the owners a shaded spot for sitting, conversation, and engaging with people walking along the street. The porch was a place between the public and private realms, where people could intermingle and establish connections. This forged a sense of shared experience and history in a neighborhood—the roots of a community.

The informal back door of the house was smaller and less embellished, placed more for efficiency and convenience than to create an impression. Since the mid–twentieth century, attached garages have become increasingly more commonplace and have actually become the norm. The convenient, casual back door is now embedded in the connection between the house and the garage. The impression of the front of the house is often overwhelmed by the dominant presence of garage doors. The strongest message this kind of house delivers is that it is friendly to *vehicles*. Once the garage doors close, the owners disappear. The community connections that once thrived on the street-facing fronts of houses now occur in the backyards, which may be open to one another or fenced. The symbolic front door has grown to become an immensely tall wall of glass, offering a glimpse of a multi-storied foyer beyond . . . imposing and impressive perhaps, but scarcely welcoming. Especially in neighborhoods without sidewalks, guests often take the path of least resistance. They enter through the garage doors, closest to where they have parked on the driveway.

As I write this, I am sitting on a comfy old overstuffed chair on the open, east facing front porch of our old craftsman style house, built in 1920. The day will

These welcoming arms of the house are expressed physically
in many forms: LONG WALLS, COLUMNS OR POSTS or fences,
paths with lighting, porches, arbors, or inviting gardens.

RIGHT: *The gabled roofs of the house and the detached garage both face the entry court.*

be hot as the sun proceeds along its high summer path, but now there is a bit of a breeze. Two cats gambol about the porch and front yard. The mail person comes up and offers me the daily missives from the world beyond. As the sun gets higher, the porch becomes increasingly shady and pleasant. Our carriage house, which contains garage and studio space, is tucked well back on the property. So it is the house, the porch, and the hefty columns of the porch that offer a welcoming greeting to the street, passersby, our guests, and to us every time we arrive home.

A front porch creates a place to be and a place for the public to arrive. But certainly not all houses require porches. Indeed, in the era of the automobile, it may be that the haven of connected backyards is a safer place for socializing and play than the street in front of the house. A porch is but one example of how a house can extend itself to the public in an inviting manner. I think of this phenomenon as the house reaching out, with open arms, in welcome.

These welcoming arms of the house are expressed physically in many forms: long walls, columns or posts or fences, paths with lighting, porches, arbors, or inviting gardens. Their common purpose is to extend a gesture of invitation to the visitor. These extensions of the house say, "Do come in . . . this way . . . please come on in!"

A red roofed cottage nestled by a Wisconsin lake exemplifies this gesture of welcome, in a slightly different manner at the "front" entry, which welcomes guests, than at the "back" entry, which is for the daily use of the family. The pieces of

this cottage are arranged carefully on the site, so that the front entry makes a strong impression as one drives up the wooded lane toward the house. The path from the detached garage and the back entry are tucked away from immediate view so that the inviting message of the front predominates.

The cottage is composed of intersecting, steeply pitched gable forms. A lower roofline sweeps across the entry side of the house. From it emerges a curved shell-shaped roof form, which is supported on two sturdy stone columns. These columns are the welcoming arms of the house. Through the windowpanes of the substantial entry doors, one can glimpse the lights within the home and the shimmering lake beyond. In temperate weather the doors are left open just as often as not. Their symmetrical plane standing open on either side of the opening, each one half of a curved top whole, reiterate the message of open arms.

In either case, the actual depth of the entry experience is definitively marked by a sequence of architectural elements, but in neither is the experience of entry overly deep or prolonged. Their purpose, instead, is to quickly usher you into the warm intimate realm of the cottage itself, and into the life of the family in it. The entries of cottages and small homes are informal in nature. Their intent is to welcome rather than to impress.

BELOW: *A desk area at the second floor landing overlooks the lake through the arched timber frames of the living room below.*

BELOW: *Although the ceiling of the living room is high, the exposed timber beams above give it a sense of human scale.*
FACING, ABOVE: *Curved* timbers and a wood ceiling overhead grace the second floor landing. An oversized window at the intermediate landing below provides lots of light.

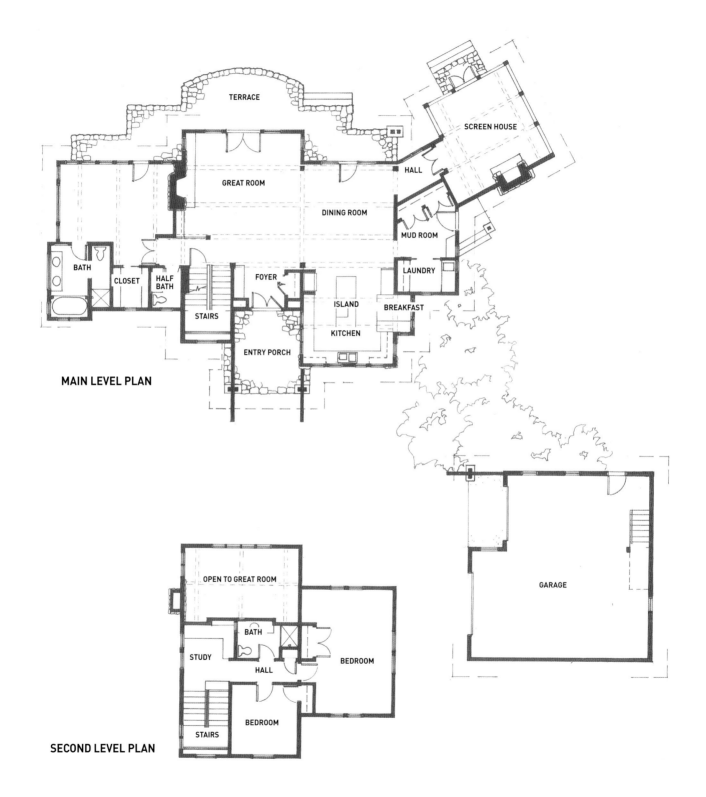

TERRACE

SCREEN HOUSE

GREAT ROOM

HALL

DINING ROOM

MUD ROOM

BATH

LAUNDRY

CLOSET

HALF BATH

FOYER

ISLAND

BREAKFAST

STAIRS

KITCHEN

ENTRY PORCH

MAIN LEVEL PLAN

GARAGE

OPEN TO GREAT ROOM

BATH

STUDY

HALL

BEDROOM

BEDROOM

STAIRS

SECOND LEVEL PLAN

The red-roofed cottage has a very charming, social, outgoing personality. It is sheltered by an animated, steeply pitched roof with many visually engaging elements: curved roof brows, dormers, a big stone chimney with a delightfully detailed cap designed by the owner, a projecting trellis, and immense solid wood beams and outriggers that reach out from the house. The outstretched arms of the main entry carry a reassuring message of strength and protection. These pieces all play a role in greeting the inhabitant or visitor. Their specific nature of form, material, and color combine to form the welcoming greeting of the house.

The welcoming greeting of a dwelling can be conveyed in many ways and is not dependent on a particular personality or style. In his book *Space, Time, and Architecture,* Sigfried Giedion asserts, "Architecture can reach out beyond the period of its birth, beyond the social class that called it into being, beyond the style to which it belongs." The essential elements of entry are a path, elements that define the path, a place of momentary shelter and repose, and a door. The expression of welcome offered may either be outgoing and exuberant or calm and reserved. The personalities of houses read differently by the ways in which architectural elements are combined at their entries. The extension of that thought might lead to speculation that the persona expressed by a house is closely related to the personality of its owners.

A house recently designed by architect Kelly Davis offers a strong, forthright expression of entry. The entry conveys the attitude, mood and personality of the home, and of the homeowners as well. Kelly is a partner with the Stillwater office of SALA Architects. He and architect Tim Old, assisted by David Ferguson, have worked together as a cohesive team for many years. The architecture they create together explores a reverence for site, structure, native materials, and rigorous detail.

The home is located on Lake Vermilion, a broad, sparkling body of water on the periphery of Minnesota's Boundary Waters Canoe Area. Both guests and owners approach the house along a curving gravel path, which extends from the detached garage sited to the northeast of the house. The house itself is a long hipped roof form with deep eaves, surrounded by dense woods of tall pine trees. The dominant ridge of the main roof is sharply contrasted by the projecting gabled form of the entry. It extends out strongly on the north side of the house, perpendicular to the main roof, extending well beyond the house to the end of the gravel path.

The entry is constructed by a series of sturdy fir posts and beams that support gabled trellis members and a gabled roof. The columns are arranged in a strong, rhythmic pattern; they are lit from below to heighten their visual impact. The pattern of columns actually extends directly into the heart of the house itself, becoming structural columns within the interior. The path they describe leads one through the foyer, into the living area, and to large windows that provide a dramatic view of the lake beyond. The full expanse of the water view is only fully perceived when one is actually directly in front of those windows.

The expression of entry here is forthright, direct, and very extroverted in character. The columns and the distant view of the lake beyond are more than inviting. This entry reaches out, and then pulls one powerfully toward and into the house. It is strong, assured, and certain in its attitude. It is both welcoming and commanding.

Inside the home, the pattern of columns ends beneath a low ceiling spanning the length of the house. As one proceeds past the edge of the low ceiling, the space opens up dramatically into a high ceiling volume, which expands to the main roof overhead. To either side are views anchored by tall stone fireplace masses. Perpendicular to the axis of the columns through the center of the house, they introduce a bold cross axis in the overall composition. The living area lies at the intersection of these spatial axes.

Generous panels of south-facing glass are interlaced with the structure that supports the large cross gable roof above.

The southern façade is a bold composition of wood, glass and stone facing the lake. The roof of the central cross gable extends out, culminating in gabled trellis members, which echo the more intimately scaled trellis at the entry to the north. Spacious decks overlooking the lake sweep to the ends of the house from either side of the powerful central gabled form.

The most important common characteristic of these entry sequences is their ability to draw people to and into the home. As we have seen, this can be accomplished in many ways. The resultant sensory attraction of the house is not dependent upon style, but on the arrangement of architectural and landscape elements that reinforce the image, location, and path to the front door. If we think of the house as a welcoming persona, the expression of entry is related to how the house

ABOVE: In the living room, immediately in front of the lakeside windows, is a spacious sitting area for two. Interior design by Talla Skogmo, of Engler/ Skogmo Interiors; construction by Mel Luloff of Luloff Construction.
FACING: The entry of the Lake Vermilion home is constructed of substantial fir columns, which are dramatically lit from below.

ABOVE: *Dining area in foreground, living room and main fireplace beyond.* RIGHT: *The lakeside façade of the house is strong and assured. The expansive windows gaze out to Lake Vermilion from beneath a sheltering roof and trellis.*

draws you to it. A person with a friendly face is immediately engaging and interesting; one feels comfortable and accepted . . . and yet eager to know more. The faces of houses are as infinitely varied as those of people. We learn early on to decipher the faces of people we meet, and seek the ones that we find most appealing and intriguing. With the same visceral and emotional equipment, we assimilate the faces and voices of houses and the messages they send us. We are instinctively most drawn to those that have the capacity to welcome us, shelter our bodies, nurture our beings, and offer the promise of happiness.

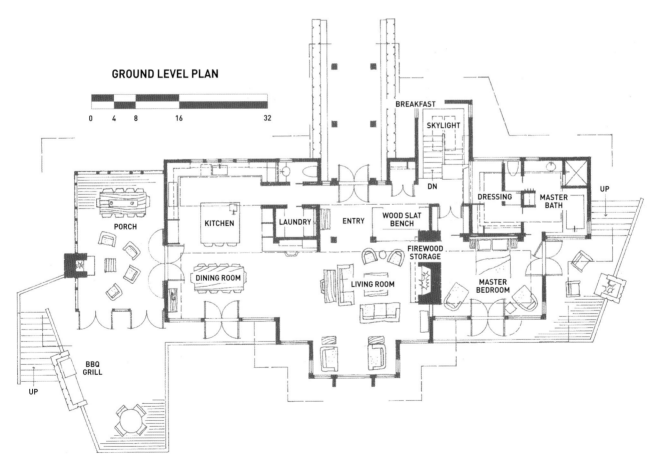

GROUND LEVEL PLAN

0   4   8   16   32

BREAKFAST

SKYLIGHT

DN

UP

PORCH

KITCHEN

LAUNDRY

ENTRY

WOOD SLAT BENCH

DRESSING

MASTER BATH

DINING ROOM

FIREWOOD STORAGE

LIVING ROOM

MASTER BEDROOM

BBQ GRILL

UP

LOWER LEVEL PLAN

0 4 8   16   32

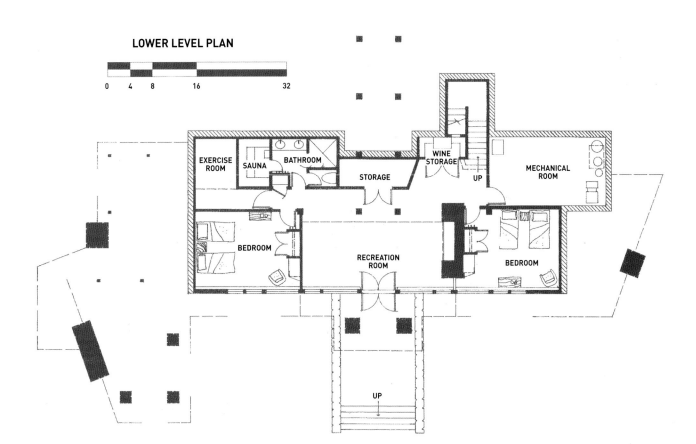

EXERCISE ROOM

SAUNA

BATHROOM

STORAGE

WINE STORAGE

UP

MECHANICAL ROOM

BEDROOM

RECREATION ROOM

BEDROOM

UP

THE HOUSE
NEXT DOOR

IN HIS BOOK *THE PLACE OF HOUSES*, Charles Moore describes different ways in which a building can fit with a site. He speaks of buildings that "merge" with the land around them as distinctly different than those that "claim" that land.

When a house is sited within the context of other neighboring homes, it may actually claim its particular piece of land, but it can also merge with the existing buildings adjacent to it, in terms of massing, rooflines, height, detail, materials, and color. There is a delicate balance between too much alikeness between neighboring properties and too much difference between them.

Sometimes neighborhoods are built up at the same time by a single builder or developer. The houses are set back the same distance from the street, are of similar size, have variations of overall form within a similar "style," and have rooflines of similar pitches but of varying shapes. Neighborhoods such as these have proliferated in American towns and cities from the eighteenth century to the present. Many of them are now treasured historic districts, displaying the ideals of home design and construction from eras past. The buildings merge with one another, forming a cohesive whole, but they differ in texture, color, landscaping, and later additions. The mark of individual owners over the years has brought about a degree of differentiation within the whole. The houses emerge as distinct identities, but they seem to be related, like the members of a family, through their shared characteristics.

I have a friend who was visiting her daughter, who had married a Frenchman. The newlyweds lived in a small village in Normandy. This village had been

established with the building of a large chateau during the Middle Ages. It also has houses built within the past year, as well as everything in between. What interested my friend was that all the dwellings went together, whether built of whitewashed walls of straw, dung and mud, of local stone, or of the most up-to-date materials. The various parts of the village all created a pleasing whole. The buildings seemed like a group of friends—large and small, old and young, sedate and boisterous—who all got along very well. Like good friends, they were respectful of each other, honored their differences, and celebrated their similarities.

The mayor emerged from his ancient farmstead and invited my friend inside. The ground floor under the house was no longer used to shelter animals, yet a lot of straw and hay remained. The mayor stuck his hand into a stack of hay bales with a hen sitting on top and pulled out a bottle of homemade Calvados, the famed local apple brandy. This lowest part of the house was protected—not too hot in summer and insulated by the walls and hay in colder weather. The onetime home for animals had become a great wine "cellar." An added benefit was that the taxman couldn't easily find the true current use of the space!

As a family changes in size or lifestyle, the house that felt "just right" in the beginning will need the grace to transform itself as life goes on, as we human beings do. The resultant changes can be a part of the process by which a group of buildings become a community.

Recent planned developments range from "beige neighborhoods"—those in which there is a great amount of sameness from building to building, which are clad in similar materials of similar neutral tones—to neighborhoods that are collections of various neo-historic styled homes. Both seem to suffer from a bit too much "sameness." But the houses change over the years as they are modified by different owners. The trees and plantings around the houses mature to a size that

ABOVE: A sketch of the 2006 Cottage Living House, in the context of its location on a city block in Evanston, Illinois. The house is designed to be a good neighbor, similar in height and mass to the neighboring homes, and clad in similar materials.
RIGHT: The streetside face of the house is a front-facing gable with shallow roof pitches—an urban bungalow.

LEFT: *Dormers create varied ceiling heights in a bedroom.*
BELOW: *An arched ceiling runs through the house along the central roof ridge. It creates a special place for a small study at the landing on the upper floor.*

is in scale with the buildings. Eventually they merge to form with a pleasing degree of differentiation within a cohesive, understandable whole.

In the summer of 2005, *Cottage Living* magazine invited me to design a cottage home for a quiet residential neighborhood near Chicago. The 2006 Idea House that resulted is a bungalow-type cottage. It is also a house I have carried around in my head for the last several years. It started out with a glimpse of an Italian cottage from a train en route from Bologna to Ravenna. It was a long, thin house with its broad side facing the sun, with big windows open to the sunlight and views on all sides. A lovely entry courtyard was framed with low garden walls of stone, which extended like embracing arms from both sides of the house. The cottage and its garden basked in the sun. I could see a bit of a wing at the back of the house. Then, as the train quickly passed, the vision disappeared. I grabbed my sketchbook. I drew plan diagrams of what I imagined the rooms inside might be.

It was a home that could easily expand or contract, depending on how far the back wing extended. In its most basic form, the cottage was a long light-filled room on the main level that contained living, eating, and cooking areas. Above were two or three bedrooms, plus a bath. The wing in the back could be added later—a flexible space that might contain a den, a main level bedroom and bath, and/or an office for a home business (as I envisioned it for my family's use, it would be an art studio.)

When *Cottage Living* approached me to design the Idea House, I immediately sought out the plans of the Italian cottage I had glimpsed. The basic concepts of the house, with its open, light-filled rooms, its entry garden, and the back wing that could grow to flexibly accommodate the needs of a family over the years seemed to suit the problem of a modest cottage on an urban site. The actual setting on a peaceful tree-canopied street in Evanston suggested an exterior form that would grow out of Chicago's historical roots and blend well with its neighbors . . . an urban bungalow. It is a house that speaks of welcome, refuge, retreat, and delight. I designed the house with Debra Kees, an architect at SALA Architects in Stillwater, Minnesota.

These are the concepts within the Idea House that we developed from those initial sketches.

1. THE LAND AND THE SUN.

The house is composed of thin pieces, one room wide, that invite light and view on many sides. The forms of the house and its garden walls create exterior rooms, which welcome its visitors on the street side and its owners as they approach from the garage through the private backyard of the house.

2. SCALE AND PROPORTION WITH THE COMMUNITY.

Scale is everything, especially in a house that is part of an existing neighborhood. The house is designed to be a good neighbor, not an overbearing one.

3. SHELTERING ROOF WINGS.

The historical precedent of the Evanston cottage is the bungalow. The bungalow (along with its ancestors in mountainous areas of Asia and Europe) is characterized by a broad, sheltering roof with deep overhanging eavelines.

Rooms within the roof: Tucking the rooms on the second floor within the volume created by the roof creates a range of interesting effects in ceiling height: low and cozy at the lower edges of the roofline, popping up at dormers, and higher in the middle of the structure, at the peak of the roof.

4. A FRONT FACING GABLE.

A child's first drawing of a house is often a house with a pitched gabled roof facing the viewer. It is an archetypal image of house and home in our culture. A front facing gable greets its inhabitants and their guests. It extends a strong sense of welcome.

5. PLACEMENT OF MATERIALS, DETAILS, AND COLOR.

Bungalows are often characterized by the classical three part model: the base (often a "hard" material, like brick or stone, which seems to be planted in and grows from the land), the mid section (a more neutral material over much of the building), and the crown, on the highest floor, under the roof. This use of materials breaks up the rather simple bungalow form into three horizontal bands, creating a sense of intimacy and human scale, as well as offering rich textural interest.

The details of Craftsman and bungalow homes are strong, hefty, and substantial. Whether or not they are actually structural in nature, they appear to "do work," to hold things up and bind them together. As well, they are gracefully proportioned and finely made, showing the mark of the human hand, of the craftsperson that made them. The *Cottage Living* house was splendidly crafted by Al Hatcher Construction of Evanston.

The color palette of the house is deep and rich, like many of the neighboring homes. It consists of a deep red brick base, chimney, and fireplace, stucco of a warm brownish gray hue, chocolate brown shingle siding and windows, and contrasting lighter brown trim, capped by a dark charcoal colored roof of asphalt shingles. The form of the house is broken into visually understandable pieces, a classical brick base, stucco mid band, and shingled crown.

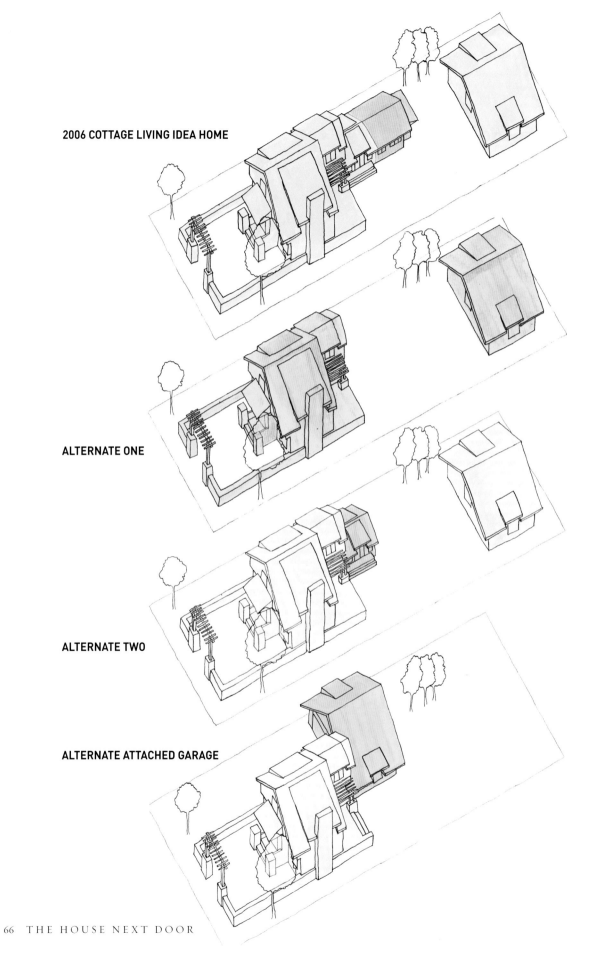

2006 COTTAGE LIVING IDEA HOME

ALTERNATE ONE

ALTERNATE TWO

ALTERNATE ATTACHED GARAGE

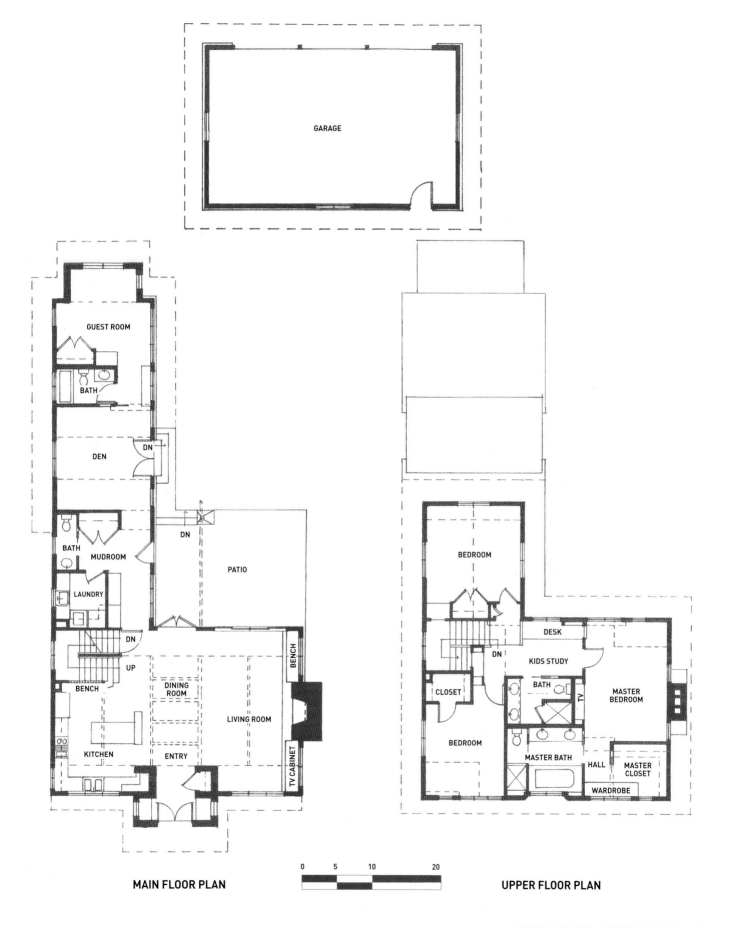

GARAGE

GUEST ROOM

BATH

DEN

DN

BATH

MUDROOM

DN

PATIO

LAUNDRY

DN

UP

BENCH

BENCH

DINING ROOM

KITCHEN

ENTRY

LIVING ROOM

TV CABINET

BEDROOM

DESK

KIDS STUDY

DN

CLOSET

BATH

TV

MASTER BEDROOM

BEDROOM

MASTER BATH

HALL

MASTER CLOSET

WARDROBE

MAIN FLOOR PLAN

0   5   10   20

UPPER FLOOR PLAN

6. THE HOUSE AND THE GARDEN.

Low walls reach out from the house to form outdoor garden rooms, which are entered through trellised arbors. Walking through the garden to the houses is a process of discovery for a guest and a constantly renewing experience that nurtures the resident. A garden can extend a sense of welcome, intrigue, and magic. Planting and weeding also provide opportunities to get to know your neighbors!

7. A COTTAGE THAT GROWS.

The *Cottage Living* house was designed for evolution over time. As architects, we often notice that clients either outgrow their homes or are outgrown by them, by building too much space in the first place. This Idea House can be built in pieces over time, as a family grows, with additions to the back wing extension. Those additions can then be used flexibly as the needs of an owner change over time. Initially, perhaps the wing might be used as a playroom and craft/hobby room or a nanny's quarters. Later, it might be used as a family room and home office. Eventually, it might evolve into a main floor bedroom and sitting area, for single-level living by empty nesters.

As in Evanston, the house can be built on a narrow lot with a detached garage. Or it can be built with a side-attached garage on a wider lot in a suburban or country setting.

Different spaces and activities are linked by common architectural elements. Living, dining, and kitchen areas are open to one another in a single flowing space, which is pulled together by a pattern of wood beams and purlins.

8. LINKING THE INSIDE TO THE OUTSIDE.

Indoor and outdoor spaces seem to flow into one another, connected by oversized doors and windows. The red brick that forms the base and chimney on the exterior extends into the house at the interior walls of the front entry, and at the fireplace, which anchors one end of the main living area. The trellis beams at the front garden entry and back patio entry are expressed as oak beams and purlins within the home.

Common activities share space, while individual activities have defined spaces. The main room, which contains the living, dining, and kitchen spaces, is designed for comfortable, casual family living and togetherness. Yet within that room, there are defined spots for use by individuals.

The forms of the house and its garden walls create exterior rooms,
WHICH WELCOME ITS VISITORS on the street side and its owners as they
approach from the garage through the private backyard of the house.

LEFT: *Low brick walls and paths of brick pavers define the plan of the garden, which was designed and created by Guillermo Castellanos.*

ABOVE: *The garden is a pleasant outdoor room, framed by brick walls, a trellis at its threshold, and shaped by plantings.*

9. DELIGHTFUL DETAILS.

The house abounds in detail, such as simple substantial millwork, built-in cabinetry, and shelves nestled into niches and perched atop window and door openings throughout the home, giving each room a sense of traditional bungalow craftsmanship, and unique spots for individual expression.

The 2006 *Cottage Living* house is an example of what might be called a seamless addition to the neighborhood. In height, width, square footage, roof forms and pitches, color, style and materials, it blends seamlessly with other homes on its block and with the community of Evanston. It achieves this "good fit" by respecting and echoing the themes and size of neighboring structures—by being like them.

ABOVE: *The dining area,*
with a view to the garden beyond.
The furnishings, lighting fixtures,
and accessories were selected by
interior designer Anne Coyle.

RIGHT: *The beamed ceiling*
hovers over the living and dining
areas, defining the spaces, yet
connecting them visually.

Living, dining, and kitchen areas are open
to one another in a SINGLE FLOWING SPACE, which is PULLED
TOGETHER by a pattern of wood beams and purlins.

LEFT: *The beamed ceiling continues over the sunny kitchen space.* BELOW: *Tall windows in the kitchen provide ample light and a view to the streetside garden. Kitchen cabinetry is combined with open shelving lit by a high transom window.*

The 2006 *Cottage Living* House is an example of what might be called a seamless addition to the neighborhood. In height, width, square footage, roof forms and pitches, color, style and materials, it blends seamlessly with other homes on its block and with the community of Evanston. It achieves this "good fit" by respecting and echoing the themes and size of neighboring structures—by being like them.

Yet a seamless addition to a neighborhood, or to a house, is not the only way of addressing the issue of what it means to build and live in an existing older neighborhood. The home of architect Eric Odor, a partner in the Minneapolis office of SALA Architects, forms a cohesive whole with neighboring structures in mass, size, and height. But an artful addition to the original house transforms it into a dwelling that delights the eye by being different from the neighboring homes.

Eric and his wife, Cory Barton, moved back to the Twin Cities from Santa Monica, California, in 1990. They quickly acquired two cats, followed shortly thereafter by the acquisition of an older home, a Dutch Colonial with a gambrel roof.

The house is located in the Linden Hills neighborhood, a vibrant, highly sought-after area of southwest Minneapolis. It is wedged in between two of the cities' lakes, Lake Calhoun and Lake Harriet, and it extends to France Avenue on the west and Forty-Seventh Street to the south. It was originally developed in the 1880s as a lake cottage community around Lake Harriet and Lake Calhoun, accessed by a streetcar line that connected the lakes with downtown Minneapolis.

Today the neighborhood is anchored by a lively commercial hub at the site of an old streetcar stop at Forty-Third and Upton Streets. The housing is an eclectic mix. Many of the old lake cottages were gradually replaced with single family homes in a variety of pre–World War II styles: Tudors, bungalows, Cape Cods, Mission style and colonials of Dutch and other persuasions.

Eric says, "We never much liked Dutch Colonials, but when we found one with maple floors and ten foot ceilings, we made an offer on the spot." Their particular Dutch Colonial was a unique case. The 30 by 20–foot house was originally built in 1905 on another site, and then moved to its current location in 1925. At some point along the way, a single car garage had been added, unfortunately with an inadequate foundation, so it kept sinking relative to the house. Eric and Cory realized that the structure of the house allowed them to remove almost every wall on the main floor,

ABOVE: A long screened porch connects the barn form to the granary/garage form and captures the summer breezes.
FACING: The streetside face of the urban farmstead.

so they quit work and gutted the entire interior in less than a month. Cory adds, "It took us years to put it back together." They started a long process of working through small projects as funds allowed.

The lot the house occupies is a large one for the area at 56 by 152 feet. A typical response these days to that size of lot is to tear down the house and build another vastly larger one, creating a big, ungainly lump between the neighboring homes in the middle of the street. But Eric and Cory (and the cats) weren't interested in a lot of expansive space; they preferred the intimate spatial quality of the existing house. They were interested, though, in a few more places to be in the house, expanding it more to the outdoors in the summer by adding a screened in porch. Eric comments, "The screened porch was a social necessity. We spent as much time as possible on the open front porch tracking the neighbors until, every summer, the mosquitoes drove us from our work."

For many years, they had been accumulating a large collection of orchids. The plants were beginning to envelop the dining room to the point that entertaining there required massive orchid relocation efforts. So an orchid room just off the dining room became part of their program list. And they needed a new garage. So Eric and Cory, who is a graphic designer, began to explore the potential of the house as a village of simple forms.

As they mused over the forms, they gradually came to the realization that what they had was not merely a Dutch colonial. It was actually—or certainly could become—a barn. The village of forms had begun to acquire an identity, that of an urban farmstead. With the removal of the existing garage, the barn needed an answering form, which became a vertical granary of corrugated metal along the southern edge of the property, roofed with a simple low-pitched gable that echoed the upper slopes of the gambrel roof. The granary accommodated their car, with room above it for storage.

A long, airy screened porch of clear cedar floats across the 10-foot separation between the two forms of the barn and the granary. The porch is both a bridge and a breezeway, hovering about 2 feet above grade at the street side, and more as the land below it descends to the backyard. Its flat roof, accessible from the main

ABOVE: *The main floor interior space is an intriguing tapestry of old and new elements.* FACING: *The back of the house facing the garden is a pleasing amalgam of glass, wood, and metal. The slope of the land affords access to a potting shed on the lower level.*

bedroom on the second floor, provides a sunny area free of rabbits and squirrels. Cory and Eric farm the roof, growing vegetables in raised containers on its slightly sloped rubber membrane surface.

The orchid room off the dining room is constructed of clear cedar and glass. The room is perched above the poured concrete walls of a potting shed a level below it. It presides over a thoughtful landscape designed by Cory. It incorporates waves of texturally varied shrubs and unusual perennials.

"We borrowed frugal and sustainable methods and materials common to farm life," says Eric. They utilized recycled and recyclable components, such as high fly-ash concrete and corrugated steel. The barn was sided with cementitious fiber-board siding. And they devised a number of means by which to harvest and control rainwater on the site. Rain chains, rain barrels, and rain gardens control and divert the water. And a 6-foot livestock tank serves as a reservoir.

Inside the home, the open interior celebrates the history of the original house and a sleek, more contemporary sensibility: art and artfulness that comes from both Eric and Cory.

The original railing on the stair to the second floor remains, but it is painted black, along with the stair risers. Cory says they think of the room as "a maple bowl." The lighting reinforces the glowing golden presence of the original maple floors, and it is amplified by the addition of an embracing wainscote of maple, detailed with exposed hardware and reveals of metal. Thin, long maple boards extend over the millwork at the heads of doors and windows. Maple shelves are tucked into hollows in the walls. Here Eric and Cory display art, sculpture, and treasured objects. Many of the furnishings, including the dining room table, were designed by Eric. They roll on the floor on casters. Both functional and curvaceous, they are a delight to the eye and the hand.

The spaces in the home are comfortable, inviting, and of intimate scale. They open to one another in a manner that feels graciously spacious, thanks in part to the 10-foot ceilings. It's easy to engage in conversation between the kitchen, dining, and living areas. All the spaces speak to each other, in the way that they are linked. And the thriving orchids, happily ensconced in their light filled alcove, speak for themselves.

MY HOME,
MYSELF

AT THE BEGINNING OF HIS INSIGHTFUL BOOK *The Architecture of Happiness,* Alain de Botton eloquently describes the persona of a house. This particular house lives on a quiet, tree-lined street. Its family has risen and clattered through their daily morning rituals, and each of the four family members has departed. The old house is left to revel in the peaceful morning. Its windows gladly receive the light, which washes the walls of the house in buttery gold. Dust motes float lazily through shafts of light. The house shifts and stretches its creaky limbs: the floors, the walls, the veins of copper and sinews of wood. The house has been a piece of its families' lives for many years, witnessing and protecting the passage of time and events that shape each family's story. De Botton goes on to relate,

"It [the house] has provided not only physical but psychological sanctuary. It has been a *guardian of identity.* Over the years, its owners have returned from periods away and, looking around them, *remembered who they were."* [my italics]

In the early part of the twentieth century, the renowned psychotherapist and philosopher Carl Jung began the process of building a house of stone. As a child, he had often crafted elaborate small versions of stone towers. (As children are wont to do, he greatly enjoyed both the building process and the drama of subsequent demolition.)

Jung spent his life examining the psyche and consciousness of mankind, both as individuals and as a collective. He extensively relied on the messages contained within his own dreams as a tool to decipher the components of the self and the psyche. In his autobiography, *Memories, Dreams, and Reflections,* he recounts a dream he had in 1909 about a house. This dream eventually shaped some of his theories of

the human psyche. In the dream, he was on an upper level of a multi-storied house. He instinctively recognized that the house was his house. The top level was a finely furnished salon. He was fascinated, curious, and impelled to explore the levels of the house below. He descended the stairs, and as he did the house became much older. The ground level was dark, with red brick walls and heavy medieval furnishings. Behind a heavy wood door lay a stone stairway leading to the basement. There he came upon a beautiful vaulted room of stone and brick, which seemed to date from Roman times. As Jung recalls, "My interest was by this time intense. I looked more closely at the floor. It was of stone slabs, and in one of those I discovered a ring. When I pulled it, the stone slab lifted, and again I saw a stairway of narrow stone steps leading down into the depths. These, too, I descended, and entered a low cave cut into the rock. Thick dust lay on the floor, and in the dust were scattered bones and broken pottery, like the remains of a primitive culture. I discovered two human skulls, obviously very old and half disintegrated. Then I awoke."

It was evident to Jung that the house represented an image of the psyche. He realized that the house, in essence, described him, and his various levels of consciousness. From this realization came his basic model of the psychic self. As he progressed downward through the house, he experienced the layers of himself, from his conscious awareness on the upper floors to the unconscious on the lower floors. In the basement cave, he found the remnants of his ancestors. He interpreted these ancient artifacts as elements of what he called the "collective unconscious," a deep intrinsic knowing common to all human beings, which we all carry within us. He identified the layers of the house in his dream as aspects of the human psyche. Later work on those concepts led him to the conclusion that the human soul is continually in the process of bringing its unconscious self into the realm of consciousness, through reflection, dreams, creative work in the form of writing, music, visual art, even the simple yet rewarding process of making things with one's hands. The study of this process of self-realization, the increasing individuation of self throughout one's lifetime, was a crucial aspect of Jung's discoveries.

Years later, in 1923, Jung decided to build a house for himself. His mother had died shortly before that time. Jung sensed within himself the need to explore his

Carl Jung expressed himself and his spirit by building his own home. The house was built in stages over a period of thirty some years. The process of his increasing self-realization is revealed in the evolving form of the building. From left: initial tower form of the Bollingen house (1923); tower with a horizontal wing (1927); complex of two towers connected by a wing (1931); addition of a courtyard and loggia (1935), and a central tower element representing his own ego-personality, which Jung added after his wife's death in 1955. Illustrations by architect Glenn Robert Lym, www.lymarch.com.

understanding of the human psyche more fully. He said, "Words and paper, however, did not seem real enough to me: something more was needed." He wanted to express himself, and his human spirit, by working with stone, allowing his ideas to evolve and grow through the process of building with his hands. He absorbed the lessons of skilled local stonemasons and participated daily in the labor of laying the stone with them. He referred to the ongoing work as a "confession of faith in stone."

The initial form of the house was a round room of stone with a hearth at its center. As it increased in height, it became a stout tower, capped with a shallow circular cone of a roof. Jung viewed it as a maternal hearth. He felt a great comfort and serenity within the round walls of that space. He began, at that point in time, to sense that the form of the structure was not only a place to be at peace with himself, but it also was a concrete expression of himself and his spirit. The house was him.

Jung continued to add pieces to the house, over a period of twelve years. The building occurred every four years. He viewed the changing forms of the building over time as reflective of changes in himself. As his process of self-realization continued, so evolved the shape of his psychic self as expressed in the stone. In 1927 he added an extended wing with a tower-like annex to the initial tower form.

Four years later, in 1931, he extended the height of the tower-like annex at the other end of the wing. He viewed this space as one for spiritual reflection and meditation. And four years after that, in 1935, he built an exterior loggia and court-yard, representing an active extension into and engagement with the natural world around him and the house.

Twenty years later, after the death of his wife in 1955, Jung felt once again prompted to continue his work on the house. He felt that the self he was expressing earlier lay primarily in the low horizontal space between the original maternal tower and the slender spiritual tower of reflection. He built another vertical element over the central space, a square tower, which he understood as expressing the evolving nature of his own spirit after his wife's death.

Jung was highly satisfied with his tower dwelling and the way in which it contained the simple rituals of daily living. He relates, "I have done without electricity, and tend the fireplace and stove myself. Evenings, I light the old lamps. There is no running water, and I pump the water from the well. I chop the wood and cook the food. These simple acts make man simple; and how difficult it is to be simple!" The tower house also provided him with a place of respite and solitude for his introverted, reflective spirit. It was a place where he felt most truly himself, remarking, "At Bollingen I am in the midst of my true life, I am most deeply myself."

Clare Cooper Marcus has extensively examined the identification of house with self in her fascinating book *House as a Mirror of Self*. In numerous interviews of subject people and their houses, she elicited profound responses regarding the nature of the relationship between oneself and one's dwelling. She found that a balance in the relationship of self and house was essential to a state of spiritual wellbeing in the individual.

Marcus' interview process was unique and insightful. She first asked people to draw a picture about their house and the meaning it had for them. Then, the picture produced was put at arm's length from the subject, and Cooper suggested that the person could engage in a conversation with their house. This often led to the house talking back to the person, and the intricacies of the relationship between the two became evident.

Some people felt so attached to their houses that the demands of carefully maintaining their houses prohibited them from a full range of interactive experience with others. Others never felt at rest or at home in any environment. Marcus relates the strong influence of early childhood experiences and memories to what one later feels to be right and necessary in a house. She describes the shifts in the perception of shelter, goals and serenity that occur in the various later phases of life, and how those changes were related to physical changes in the house itself. As well, she examines the impact experienced by people who lose a house, and the challenges faced by those who set up housekeeping together, when they attempt to find the ways in which their house can be expressive of both of them.

Marcus observed that the particular phenomenon of house as a reflection of self was only somewhat evident in the exterior of the house, the social face that the house displayed to the public. Only a relatively small number of people have the opportunity to express themselves by actually building a house. Thus, she found that the interior of the home was the main focus of most people's yearning to express themselves through their home. This was accomplished through the assemblage of furnishings, paintings, photographs, personal collections, sculpture, pots, plants, souvenirs of travel, textiles, floor coverings, curtains, color, patterns, light, and texture. It was also evident in the way people displayed or concealed the stuff of everyday living: books, tools, computers, hobbies, clothing, jewelry, bed linens, towels, lamps, musical instruments, cookware, dishes, and cooking utensils.

Jung had come to a similar conclusion. In the same sense in which he identified the form of his tower dwelling with his psychic self, Jung further came to the understanding that the objects made manifest by creative endeavors were

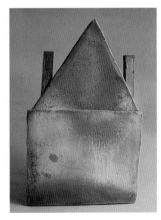

☞ *Three house pots by Wayne Branum.*

Three tower buildings by Wayne Branum.

identifiable with the spirit of the artist or creator who brings them forth. These creative endeavors were pieces of the creator's unconscious, brought into the light of consciousness by the act of making.

I have found that the houses of very creative people display this phenomenon most aptly. Artists in particular seem very comfortable surrounding themselves with their work and their "stuff": with objects that capture their interest, things that display their passions and pastimes, and everyday items from their daily routines. They often weave these elements together, melding the pieces into the environment around them so that the resultant whole becomes an ever-evolving portrait of themselves, their lives, and their spirits. The association of art form, architectural form, and self is even more evident when the artist is also an architect.

A house and studio designed by architect and artist Wayne Branum, one of the partners at SALA architects, is an intriguing combination of architecture and art. Wayne is a potter as well as an architect: his potting studio is a part of the complex that makes up the dwelling he shares with Ann Routier on a western Wisconsin hilltop. Here, the form of the architecture and the form of the art seem related. They clearly seem to spring from the same maker, the same creative roots.

Wayne's pots come in many forms. Some are purely and wonderfully functional: bowls, platters, plates, cups and other vessels, simple thrown forms in satisfying earthen tones of rust, amber, brown, and black. The pots are fired in a large wood-fired kiln in the studio. This process of salt firing creates variation of hue and texture which richly enhances the final surface. A pot that is anticipated to be rust in color can come out of the kiln in tones of cream, tan, amber, red, and brown. Often the pots receive a bit of embellishment, a quick, almost calligraphic organic gesture or a playful, graphic combination of strokes or stripes that form a loose grid on the body of the vessel.

Other pots are created out of slabs of clay. They often take the shape of abstract built forms; in fact, Wayne calls them house pots. The houses are of all sizes, from little triangular houses with steeply pitched roof/lids to vertical towers with more subdued sloped roof/lids. Their surfaces are embellished with little repeated geometric shapes, or lines parallel to the slope of a lid. Sometimes one side of the house pot might be entirely of surprisingly bright, contrasting hues, reverting to darker, more subdued tones on the other side. The house pots combine great sensitivity to form and proportion. And they are possessed of a joyous spirit. They emanate the casual carefree grace that might be found in a child's house drawings. They are not only pots and houses but also personas. Each of them portrays another aspect of self.

These are themes Wayne has worked with for many years. If all his house pots were assembled in one place, they would be a huge community of related forms, each different in itself, but definitely a member of the same family.

The houses he creates as an architect often seem to be members of the very same family, or at least close relations. They are simple, abstract forms knit together in strong combinations. The contrasting pieces mesh in satisfying but slightly unexpected relationships to one another. Tall vertical pieces intersect with lower forms that hug the ground.

His own house is a good example. The site of the house is a windswept hill overlooking undulating fields of Wisconsin farmland. One's first impression of the house from a road down in the valley is a quick glimpse of a tower. The tower gazes over the treetops, quietly observing the fields and woods that stretch below.

A steep, wooded driveway ascends the hill; the tree trunks at its sides seem just close enough together to provide a bit of reassurance that you won't roll down the hill between them. The driveway's path curves sharply to the right as

RIGHT BELOW: *View towards the fireplace.*

The Hickman House.

The interior of the home is a quiet, calming space, filled with light from large windows to the south and expansive views of the sheltering woods to the southwest. A low-ceilinged entry area is shaped by a bench on one side and shelves of pots, books, and art on the other. Immediately to the right, a stair begins the ascent to the domain of the tower. As one steps just beyond the entry, the ceiling rises to a span of clerestory windows. Some of the glass faces the exterior, admitting northern light. Adjacent panes of glass connect the room on the main level to an office area on the second level of the tower, allowing borrowed light and views between those spaces.

This main room contains the kitchen, eating, and living areas together, in a single space. The kitchen is tucked away from immediate view by the wood walls around the refrigerator situated at the end of the island. An inviting living area inhabits the opposite corner, with comfortable furnishings and a built-in couch gathered around a hearth. The entire room is crafted of warm woods, bright windows, and a stained concrete radiant floor that flows between the spaces. The sloped ceiling overhead is of the same galvanized metal that clads the exterior of the home. The curved striations of the metal catch the light from the windows and distribute it into the volume of the space. The combination of materials is intriguing; it feels both warm and cool at the same time.

The private realm of the bedroom is located down a short hallway to the southeast. And another private realm, that of the tower, inhabits the northwest corner of the house. It stands like a stalwart protective presence, foiling the dominant northwest winds that pummel the top of the hill. The stairs of the tower wind around its perimeter, accessing first a semi-private second level, an office space that doubles for the use of visiting family members or overnight guests. Then, a final flight ascends to the seclusion of the room at the top of the tower. This place in the house is magical. Flooded with light and panoramic views of the surrounding countryside, it is a place for reflection, repose, and creative work. South-facing doors open to a tiny balcony under the sheltering eave of the roof above. The balcony projects from the wall of the tower. It gathers light, warmth, and seasonal breezes, while peacefully contemplating the valley below.

Several years ago I became acquainted with David Hickman and his wife, Linda. David is a sculptor. His sculptures are of wood, stone, steel, and glass. They range in size from small, intimately scaled pieces to massive kinetic ones that launch themselves above the treetops. He has received numerous awards for his work and for his and Linda's work within the artistic community in Dallas. In 2004 the Texas Commission on the Arts selected him as the Texas State Artist, and he was named artist of the year in 2005 by the Dallas chapter of the American Institute of Architects. David and Linda live in a ranch-style home in the midst of an extensive and wondrous sculpture garden populated by David's work and that of other sculptors.

"The shape of the building, THE WALLS AND
THE ANGLES where they meet, IS A RESPONSE to how these two
people live their lives with each other, to their give and take."

FACING: *A path punctu-
ated by metal tree forms creates
a promenade in the sculpture
courtyard. The courtyard
culminates at the gallery space
beyond.* BELOW: *The courtyard
is populated by figural sculptures,
such as this piece by David.*

It was Linda Hickman who first spotted their future home, during an hour-long lunch break nearly thirty years ago. She and David were planning on being married in a year. The cottage was a small, unassuming ranch house built in 1941. It was located on an overgrown acre of land in a Dallas suburb. A dense thicket of brush and trees covered the southern end of the site. The house looked a bit tired and worn, but Linda immediately sensed its potential. Recalling that day, she says, "I immediately thought that David could make this beautiful."

They moved into the house in 1981. Over the ensuing twenty-eight years, David and Linda have transformed the house and its surrounds. Their initial step was to clear the thicket at the far southern end of the site, where they built a spacious 3,200-square-foot studio space for David. They added a main bedroom and bath and transformed the interior of the home. Recently, with the help of architect Bentley Tibbs, they expanded the kitchen and added a gallery space adjacent and open to the kitchen. David has indeed made the place beautiful. In the course of doing so, he and Linda have created a living portrait of themselves, their work, and their lives together.

Clare Cooper Marcus suggests that the outside of a house displays the public persona of those who live in it and how they wish to be perceived by others. In contrast, the inside of the house offers a picture of the owners' inner selves. At first glance, as one approaches from the street, the outside persona of David and Linda's dwelling is still the mild-mannered ranch house. It is modestly clad in wood stained dark brown and peers out from behind a screen of tall flowering crepe myrtle trees that partially mask the identity behind them, kind of like the frames of Clark Kent's glasses. But as one approaches, one cannot help but notice the unexpected presence of three bold, overscaled bicycles, abstract and brightly colored, which seem to have briefly interrupted their flight to touch down on the ridge of the garage roof. Their whimsical grin greets you; it's almost impossible not to smile at the sight of them. Just to the left of the path to the entrance, a set of three angular massive limestone slabs are set into the earth. Their gentle, stalwart presence nudges the visitor to the front door, along a path lined with colorful plantings. When the front door opens, one is immediately in another realm: the defining realm of the interior self.

The living areas are at once an incredibly free yet thoughtful collision of color, texture, and form. Sculpted figures of stone, wood, and metal gracefully inhabit the spaces. The walls are lined with paintings and drawings by artist friends. They are painted in strong, vivid tones, inspired by the color palette architect Ricardo Leggoretta used at the Latino Cultural Center in Dallas.

Over the fireplace mantel is a concertina of carved wood, frozen in a joyously expanded pose. David plays the concertina, accordion, and dulcimer. A collection of his instruments is arranged in the next room, a comfy place for relaxation lined with red leather sofas. Here a monumental pair of carved wood columns and a

lintel, from Michoacan, Mexico, enshrine a large flat-screen TV, in a gesture which humorously acknowledges the prominent status of the television in daily life.

In 2003, David and Linda sought the advice of an architect to help them add space to their house. They were referred by a friend to Bentley Tibbs, a residential architect who lives nearby. Bentley recalls the first time he visited with David and Linda to discuss their project. "Immediately upon stepping into the house, I knew I was entering David and Linda's world," he declares. "The house *was* David and Linda." David and Bentley collaborated on the design of the remodeled kitchen, adding an extension beyond it that is linked to a gallery space proposed by the architect. Although they had not initially planned such a space, David and Linda readily appreciated what it might add to their house—a lofty, open, light-filled space in which they could exhibit art, entertain guests, play music, and display David's instruments.

The new gallery opens on both its north and south sides to extensive outdoor garden/patio spaces that connect the gallery, house, and studio. Architect Bentley Tibbs describes it as "seemingly simple," in that at first glance the form of the addition seems to be an airy cube with a shallowly sloped roof. But the plan is actually 10 to 20 degrees off orthogonal at all of the corners. Two particular kinds of walls converge to form the enclosure. A pair of the walls are of weathered cedar, with deep horizontal fins that wrap around corners like corrugations of wood. Cradled between the wood walls and the house is a third wall of galvanized metal. Tibbs thinks of the two wall types as exemplifying David (the wood) and Linda (the metal). Their union in forming the space describes the relationship between them. Tibbs remarked, "The shape of the building, the walls and the angles where they meet, is a response to how these two people live their lives with each other, to their give and take."

As important as the wood and the metal is a third element—light. The initial design for the gallery featured large plate glass windows at both the north and south sides. Bentley proposed another thought: to puncture both walls with a freely arranged assortment of window openings, twenty-seven in all. David was immediately drawn to the idea because the separate windows frame the light and view like picture frames, and, as he says, "The picture is constantly changing."

The gallery space is a kind of hub from which all the other spaces and elements flow. The garden to the south has taken shape as a long promenade within a sheltered courtyard. One proceeds from the gallery to a small covered outdoor dining area of posts and beams: its materials and manner of construction echo the original ranch house. Beyond the covered porch, a path extends between an ordered arrangement of large, abstract metal tree forms. It leads to the studio at the opposite end of the courtyard.

Along the path one encounters figural sculptures, both large and small, by David and other artists. These pieces act like personalities that greet visitors as they proceed along the courtyard path. One has the sense of being within a wondrous and

fantastical realm, simultaneously inside and outside, populated by unusual and beautiful beings, fountains, and plantings.

The garden space to the north of the gallery is fashioned of a large, encompassing circle, presided over figural sculptures arranged around it, facing towards the center of the circle. In the midst of the circle is an enormous stone table and benches composed of heavy stone slabs. A bronze figure of a thoughtful, reflective seated woman rests atop the table. She sets a quiet, introspective mood in this secluded circular garden enclosure.

The inside of the gallery space opens to the kitchen. The walls of the gallery are painted in deep hues of Navajo red and marigold. An organically formed flowing mosaic fireplace, crafted by David, anchors one corner of the room. It suggests the eruption of a volcano, with colorful lava swelling down its sides, flowing into a stone mosaic river on the floor. The shape of the fireplace was roughly built of plywood and then covered with wire mesh and mortar, which was then clad with pieces of ceramic tiles cut to size in David's studio. Its fluid shapes and hot, intense colors seem like the essence of the fire they enclose.

A comfortable seating arrangement is grouped near the fireplace, facing back into the kitchen. A changing array of sculptures and artifacts stand silhouetted against the vivid walls, framed by the collection of window shapes and illuminated by light passing through them. The gallery floor is of poured concrete, embedded in spots with details of mosaic fragments.

The kitchen has been transformed into the flamboyant sister of its pale original self. The original windows and millwork were retained. New cabinets and cupboards were built in the same spirit as the original cabinetry. All these wood surfaces are painted a brilliant turquoise. The soffit area above the cupboards is painted a deep magenta. The color is a perfect foil for the assorted baskets and colorful pottery displayed against it. The walls are bright marigold, and the commercial rubber floor and backsplash tiles at the stove and sink are cobalt blue. David made a stainless steel top for a simple utilitarian steel tool storage cart. It serves as an island and tabletop in the center of the brightly hued space.

A venerable old Chambers stove nestles into a tiled corner. Above it in the cobalt tiled corner are two painted tiles depicting a pair of flamenco dancers. They are a gift from a former student of David's. Their gay swirling poses seem to embody the spirit of the entire kitchen space. It is one of the most cheerful, joyous kitchens I've ever been in. Like many places in the Hickmans' house and gardens, it is delightful to enter and very difficult to leave.

In the evening, the gallery windows glow like cut openings in a lantern. Their randomly scattered shapes lend a captivating luminescence to the courtyard. Linda remarks, "To me, the gallery is like a little jewel box." The Hickmans' house, studio, gallery, and courtyard are the setting not only for precious gems of artwork, but also for the evolving life David and Linda have created together.

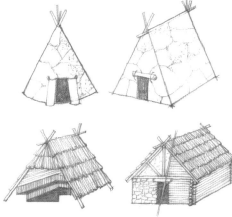

THE WINGS OF THE ROOF

⟨⟩ WHEN HUMAN BEINGS FIRST sought shelter they found it in places provided by nature. A cave or the widespread branches of a tree offered a sheltering roof overhead. When early man began to make his own shelter, he fashioned huts from tree branches lashed together, covered over by reeds or thatch, and earth or sod over that. Hunters and shepherds stretched animal skins over wooden supports, assembling the first tents.

One of the most basic forms of man-made roofs is a simple tent: a single sheet of protective material, propped up in the center and tied down to the ground on either side. The central supports provide the volume for a high, inhabitable spot in the middle, and the slanted wings of fabric on either side shed the elements away from the protected area. One can think of the tent as the mother of all roofs. We physically and emotionally understand its intimate shelter as a direct extension of our bodies, in a gesture with arms spread out, sheltering those below. As children we might have sensed that kind of wondrous protection in a private spot under a table draped by a cloth. The roof keeps us secure, warm and safe, in our own haven. It casts its protective wings about us, like the sheltering arms of a loved one much bigger than oneself. That, in the most elemental sense, is the message of the roof.

Mankind has created all sorts of sheltering roof forms, depending on the nature of the materials at hand and the kind of protection that the elements demanded.

A great many of these forms are variations of tent-like shapes. The gabled form suggested by the homely pup tent has been reinterpreted in countless ways by different cultures throughout history. It speaks to us in the ancient tongue of an

PERSPECTIVE.

DESCRIPTION.

For explanation of all symbols (* † etc.) see supplement page 120.

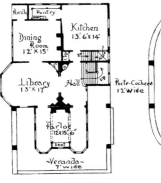

FIRST FLOOR.

GENERAL DIMENSIONS: Width, 33 ft. 6 ins., not including porte-cochere; depth, including veranda, 39 ft.

HEIGHTS OF STORIES: Cellar, 7 ft.; first story, 9 ft. 6 ins.; second story, 9 ft.

EXTERIOR MATERIALS: Foundation and veranda, etc., stone; first story, clapboards; second story, gables and roofs, shingles.

INTERIOR FINISH: Three coat plaster, hard white finish. Plaster centers in parlor, dining-room, library and hall of first story. Flooring, N. C. pine throughout. Trim, white wood. Main staircase, ash. Bathroom and kitchen wainscoted. Chair-rail in dining-room. Picture molding in principal rooms and hall of first story. All interior woodwork grain filled and finished with hard oil varnish.

SECOND FLOOR.

COLORS: All clapboards, light terra-cotta. Trim, dark terra-cotta. Shingling on second story, gables, etc., stained red. Roof shingles, oiled. Outside doors and sashes, also veranda floor and ceiling, finished with hard oil.

ACCOMMODATIONS: The principal rooms and their sizes, closets, etc., are shown by the floor plans. Cellar under the whole house. Sink, range and boiler in kitchen. Bathroom, with complete plumbing. Laundry, with two set wash-tubs, in cellar. Open fireplaces in dining-room, parlor, hall and library. Wide portière opening connects dining-room and library. Sliding doors connect library, parlor and hall. Hall contains very pretty staircase. Butler's pantry connecting kitchen and dining-room, contains sink, dresser and china closet. Linen closet in second story hall.

COST: $4,500, including mantels, range or heater. The estimate is based on † New York prices for materials and labor. In many sections of the country the cost should be less.

Price of working plans, specifications, detail drawings, etc., . $45.

Price of †† bill of materials, ... 15.

FEASIBLE MODIFICATIONS: General dimensions, materials and colors may be changed. Cellar may be reduced in size or wholly omitted. Laundry may be omitted and tubs transferred to kitchen. Brick-set range may be introduced in kitchen. Sliding doors may be omitted and portière openings substituted. Attic may be finished for two rooms.

The price of working plans, specifications, etc., for a modified design varies according to the alterations required, and will be made known upon application to the Architects.

Address, CO-OPERATIVE BUILDING PLAN ASSOCIATION, Architects, 203 Broadway and 164–6–8 Fulton Street, New York, N. Y.

94

FACING: *Shingle style house in Shoppells Catalog of Home Plans, circa 1880s.* ABOVE: *This simple, strong roof form has been an enduring inspiration for countless homes, both by architects and by vernacular builders.*

archetype. We understand what it says in a visceral manner, through the way our bodies sense its protective gesture.

Think for a moment of the peaked, triangular form of a tent over a rectangular form beneath it. In its abstracted form it becomes a large triangle, hovering over a smaller square below. This is one of the most enduring and widely recognized symbols of home.

Frank Lloyd Wright surely recognized this when he used a particularly strong, hovering, protective roof form on the public street side of his own house and studio in Oak Park, Illinois. He lived there for twenty years, from 1889 to 1909, with his first wife, Catherine Tobin; they raised six children there. Wright used the building as a laboratory for testing his early architectural concepts. In fact, the predominant triangular roof form originally contained his drafting room until the studio annex was completed in 1898.

Where did this house come from? What are its roots? The excellent book *Shelter*, edited by Lloyd Kahn, declares, "Many architects and designers do not acknowledge their sources. Much that passes for invention or innovation is actually misappropriated (and often highly publicized) work of others. This tends to inhibit architecture students or designers, as the achievements of the 'masters' appear stunning when out of the context of their historical roots. Every creative person has roots." The Wright studio home is basically in the Shingle Style, with deep brown shingle siding and roof shingles that seem to merge into one another, creating the sense of a pure triangular volume. A broad lunette window rests gracefully below the peak of

Architect Frank Lloyd Wright used a strong triangular roof form to shelter his own family home and studio in Oak Park, Illinois.

the gable. Vincent Scully, in *The Shingle Style,* notes the similarity and possible historical influence of a Shingle Style house designed by Bruce Price, built in Tuxedo Park, New York, in 1886. Shingle-style homes were much in vogue at the time; their walls and roofs were basic geometric volumes clad with wood shingles on all surfaces, lending them a satisfying simplicity of form that their High Victorian neighbors lacked. House plan catalogs of the era abound with designs featuring simple massive, triangular gable forms overhanging submissive sheltered walls below them. But one wonders if the simple language of the shapes of the legendary Froebel blocks that Wright played with as a child were not even more influential. Perhaps he returned to the house symbol he had discovered then, the large triangle hovering over the smaller square below it, and simply interpreted it in the idiom of the time.

Architect Katherine Hillbrand, a partner in the Stillwater office of SALA Architects, combined the big triangular roof with a perpendicular gabled roof that seems to whimsically kick up its skirts on one side. The cottage, at the edge of a lake near Stillwater, Minnesota, was a complete transformation of a small two-story cabin that originally stood there. The original cabin stood at the crest of a very gentle slope down to the lake. Hillbrand sank the addition a few feet down into the land, so that it nestles down into the site.

She wrapped the rectangular form of the cabin with another form to create the addition, which contains the entry, a dining area in a window-filled nook, and a living area in the dominant gable end facing the lake. The eaves of the big red triangular roof descend down close to the ground, making the height of the house more approachable and less intimidating. Like powerful limbs, overscaled support columns bear the triangular volume above. They are another humanizing element;

In this lakeside home by
designed by architect Katherine
Hillbrand with Ann Hauer, an
inviting entry is sheltered by
roof wings that extend out from
the house. Stone walls retain the
earth at the side, reinforcing the
feeling of protection.

their profiles suggest the curve of a thigh. The house was built by Mark Youngdahl as his own family home.

The entry to the home is enticing, inviting, and slightly mysterious. It beckons the visitor along a winding stone path, through an extension of the roof form that is knit around a corner of the cottage. On the right side of the entry, a stone retaining wall holds back the higher ground around it, giving the sense that as you enter the house, you are entering the earth itself.

In 1997, *Life* Magazine challenged our architectural firm, then called Mulfinger, Susanka, Mahady & Partners, to design a moderately sized house for family living, a structure that one "needn't be a millionaire to own." They had been drawn to the thoughts expressed by Sarah Susanka, a co-founder of the firm, in her book *The Not So Big House: A Blueprint for the Way We Really Live.* Several architects from our firm worked on schematic, conceptual design alternatives for them. They selected the design I had done, which was based on a simple cube-like historic house type called the four-square, with four rooms up and four rooms down. I capped the foursquare plan with a broad triangular volume overhanging the plan cube below. The large triangle bore symmetrical window and door openings, suggesting an anthropomorphic face.

A team of nine architects from our firm developed my design into two houses, the Basic house and the Upgrade house, which we dubbed "the Whole Nine Yards." As their names suggest, the Basic house was smaller and more affordable, while the Whole Nine Yards was larger and more detailed. Both homes have covered front porches, which extend an invitation to neighbors. The porch provides the visitor with a bit of shelter and respite and the homeowners with a seasonal living space.

We aimed to MAKE THE MOST OF THE SQUARE FOOTAGE available
by making all the spaces useable on a daily basis,
and open to one another, providing a feeling of spaciousness.

LEFT: *The big sheltering roof of the Whole Nine Yards House covers an entry porch below. Its symmetrical, ordered façade is clad in cedar siding and sawn cedar shingles. A balcony off the front bedrooms projects from the gable, and a quizzical face emerges from the shingles at the peak of the roof.* ABOVE: *The simple, symmetrical placement of window pairs and entry door below reads clearly as a face. Bold colors create a pleasing contrast between the big roof form above and the main floor rooms tucked below.*

A big triangular roof hovers over each house, creating a sense of stability and substance. The facelike façade sends a reassuring greeting of welcome.

The face of the Basic House is simple, clear, and unadorned. The team of architects who worked on it, headed by Jean Rehkamp Larson, were inspired by farmhouses and Shaker design. It is clad in clapboard and painted in bold contrasting hues, which further differentiate the floating triangular top from the main floor areas below it. The Basic House was built by Kyle Hunt and Partners. The Whole Nine Yards house is more textural and elaborate in its development, with balconies that emerge from the triangular gabled roof form on both front and back, and dormers that bring light into the second floor rooms. This team of architects, which I led, interpreted the house in a manner that had its roots in historic Shingle Style and Modern Craftsman homes. Built by Derrick Construction, the house is sided with a mixture of sawn shingles and clapboard, and a hefty stucco base anchors the house to the site below it. Its exterior details of wood and metal are shaped in a distinctive manner, introducing a hint of modernity to the historic form. A whimsical face peeks out under the peak of the gabled roof.

Inside, both houses are laid out similarly, with an emphasis on family-oriented daily living. We aimed to make the most of the square footage available by making all the spaces useable on a daily basis. The old four-square four-room plan on the main level was opened up to create a connected, flowing space that contains living, dining, and kitchen areas. This technique brings family members together while providing

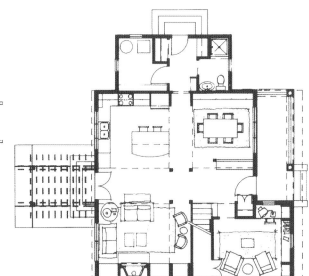

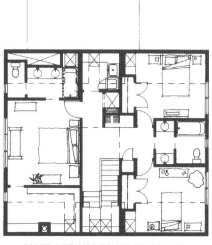

MAIN AND UPPER LEVEL PLANS, BASIC HOUSE

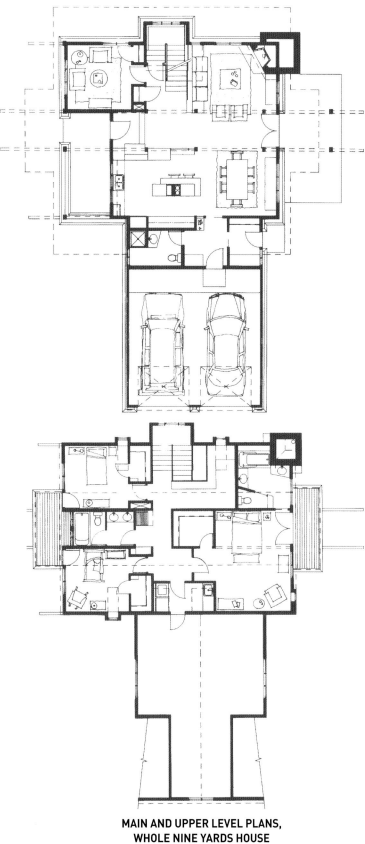

MAIN AND UPPER LEVEL PLANS, WHOLE NINE YARDS HOUSE

FACING ABOVE: *The open floor plan of the Basic House revolves around a central quadrant of columns.* FACING BELOW: *The dining area is screened from the entry by a gracefully curved partition wall.*

a feeling of spaciousness. But a private fourth room, which we called the away room, kept its walls. This cozy room could be used flexibly as an office, a separate spot for watching television or playing music, a den, or an additional bedroom. It provided the opportunity for some quiet seclusion amidst the open plan. A well accessorized mudroom with closets, a bench, a cabinet for sorting and storing mail, and an adjacent half bath connects the family entry from the garage to the main level living spaces.

On the second floor the rooms are tucked within the volume created by the big roof. They have sloped ceilings at their outer edges, creating a cozy sense of enclosure. Two of the four foursquare plan rooms were combined into a main bedroom suite with a bath and walk-in closet. The other two rooms are children's bedrooms, sharing a bathroom. Both homes feature an open unfinished space in the roof above the garage for future expansion.

In keeping with their respective themes, the interior finishes are colorful and simple in the Basic House. The Whole Nine Yards House is more richly attired, with more wood on the walls and ceilings, more elaborate detail, and more luxurious amenities throughout.

The interior finishes
ARE COLORFUL AND SIMPLE
in the Basic House.

The Whole Nine Yards House IS MORE RICHLY ATTIRED, with more wood on the walls and ceilings, more ELABORATE DETAIL, and more luxurious amenities throughout.

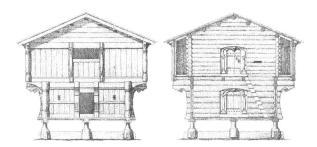

THE HANDCRAFTED HOME

IF WE THINK OF A HOUSE AS A WELCOMING PERSONA, we might liken its exterior materials, its wall cladding and roofing, to its clothing. We might then begin to conceive of the detail and ornamentation of a building as the building's jewelry.

The relationship of ornament to architecture, like that of jewelry to the human form, is one of contrast, visual emphasis, and embellishment. It can emphasize and strengthen architectural themes and can be read at many scales. At a human scale, it appeals to tactile, aesthetic, and physical senses. It also conveys symbolic and metaphoric meaning, appealing to man's spiritual sense.

In his book *Timeless Way of Building,* Christopher Alexander describes the relationship of ornament to the form that receives it. He tells of a simple wood bench. The maker of the bench senses that it could be even more "just right." He adds a pattern of hearts carved out of the wood on the back of the bench. The ornament of the bench, its jewelry, flows freely from the hand of the maker into the bench and completes it as a whole. It implies the hand of the maker and invites the touch of those who use the bench. And it conveys a simple, sweet message in the symbolism of the heart shape.

During the late nineteenth century, architects and designers sought to systematize methods of ornamentation by separating it from its stylistic roots. When ornament was separated from its role within a particular style, the "free eclecticism" of gingerbread-festooned Victorian houses resulted. In *The Grammar of Ornament,* published in 1865, Owen Jones described principles for the arrangement of color and form in the composition of ornament. The illustrations that accompany

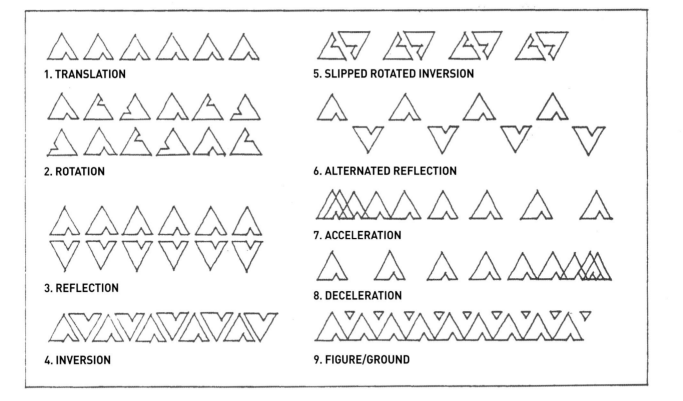

1. TRANSLATION

2. ROTATION

3. REFLECTION

4. INVERSION

5. SLIPPED ROTATED INVERSION

6. ALTERNATED REFLECTION

7. ACCELERATION

8. DECELERATION

9. FIGURE/GROUND

Owen's essay show an ornamental design involved a number of manipulations of a basic unit, a geometric shape. He repeated the unit, flipped it upside down or sideways, and pushed the units closer together or farther apart to achieve different compositions by varying the amount of negative space between the pieces.

Owen Jones thought of the process of ornamentation as systematic and logical. Louis Sullivan would later develop a similar system with natural forms. However, either approach was a logical *system* within itself, increasingly independent of and applied to architectural form. This is inherently quite different from the intuitive expression of the carved hearts on the bench described by Alexander. The hearts are in and of the bench; either alone would be incomplete. And the logical systematic approach was of the intellect, while the carved bench was the expression of the senses and feeling.

At the beginning of the twentieth century, the industrial revolution introduced the concept of technology as a new basis for society's ways of thinking, working, and building. Building methods based on new technology caused a complete reanalysis of the purpose of architecture. Architectural design was based on program, function, systems, modularity, and the direct expression of structure and materials. The principal aesthetic and symbolic metaphor of Modern architecture became the machine. When Corbusier stated, "A house is a machine for living," he brought the metaphor of the machine directly to the concept of dwelling.

The early Modernists were convinced that science and technology would completely transform the world for the better, and the buildings they produced were radically different from those of their predecessors. Traditional forms and their

A rational system of ornamentation described by Owen Jones in an 1865 essay. This approach tended to separate ornament from architectural expression, so that it became an applied afterthought rather than an inherent component of the building. PREVIOUS SPREAD (illustration): *A historic Norwegian stave loft building.*

❧ In the original Dairy Building at Iowa State University, the sculptural artwork of Christian Petersen melds with the architecture of the building. The bas-relief terra-cotta figures proceed through the arched openings in the building, depicting the history of the dairy industry. Here, the artwork is integral to the architecture. It amplifies the theme of the repeated arched openings and tells a story.

inherent symbolism were completely shunned by the mainstream of Modern thinking. They were rejected for new, innovative forms directly related to function. Ornament was regarded as unnecessary, functionless excess.

The intellectual fervor that spurred the Early Modernists gradually dissipated as the ideas of the masters were handed over to subsequent generations. Some of their buildings were sublimely beautiful in their unadorned simplicity, but they demanded an extremely high level of skill and precision in both design and construction. When absorbed and reinterpreted by the general building culture, the notions of system and modularity led to the prioritization of efficiency and economy in construction. The message conveyed by the form and ornament of a building was lost. A blight of bland, monotonously similar, cheaply constructed structures has resulted. These buildings are devoid of expression and lacking in the qualities of human scale and overall proportion of buildings of the past. If, as Vitruvius claimed, "Well building hath three conditions: commodity, firmness and delight," these buildings are simply *not well*.

Eventually, the optimism of advertising slogans like "Better living through chemistry" gave way to extreme concern over the scars that uncontrolled and misused technology left on the environment. Modern technology was increasingly seen as alienating man from himself and his surroundings.

Since then, architecture has become increasingly less dependent on the rational minimalism of early Modernism. Architects are exploring new vocabularies of form that have the potential to recapture a sense of meaning and human values in buildings. They spring from diverse sources: historical precedent, sustainable

building practices, self expression, memory, the psychology of place, and the art and craft of building itself.[1]

Several years ago I designed a project for a small cottage dwelling on Madeline Island, which is located in the northern waters of Lake Superior. The homeowners, Mark and Bonnie, are avid sailors, and they had great appreciation for the careful craftsmanship and the economy of form and space in their sailboat, *Dulcínea*. Also, they

1. Robert Jensen and Patricia Conway. *Ornamentalism: The New Decorativeness in Architecture and Design.* New York: Clarkson N. Potter Inc., 1982.

felt emotionally drawn to the work of architect Edwin Lundie, particularly his cabins on the northern shore of Lake Superior. Lundie practiced in Minnesota for roughly fifty years, from the 1920s through the 1960s. He delighted in the use of the vernacular, regional building forms from various cultures. His lake cabins in Minnesota are small, expressive structures that exhibit a Scandinavian influence in their method of construction and detailing. Lundie may have been inspired by the stave loft buildings of Norway. These were simple, gabled structures of heavy wood posts and beams. The sturdy wood members were shaped and carved with symbolic ornamentation.

A typical stave loft structure had only one room per level and a cantilevered gallery on the second level. They were originally used as "treasuries" for grain storage above and animals below. In the summer, they served as sleeping quarters.

Lundie's North Shore cabins are chunky, heavy, and substantial in character. Their massive carved posts and beams seem unabashedly more than equal to their structural task. The overscaled structural components give an immensely solid, reassuring feel to the cabins. The buildings seem like wise spirits of the woods and water; one senses a little magic in them. They are dwellings that seem to have been there forever, and will so remain. They are most definitely houses that greet their owners and visitors with a resounding, welcoming hello.

⮑ FACING: *This cabin on the Brule River in northern Wisconsin was designed by Edwin Lundie in the 1960s. It employs the timber frame method of building.* RIGHT: *The guest cabin porch demonstrates a kinship to Norwegian stave buildings, in both proportion and building technique.*

The homeowners hoped the COTTAGE would have the
WELCOMING, MAGICAL COME-HITHER feeling of
Lundie's cabins on the North Shore.

⮞LEFT: The kitchen nestles under a lowered ceiling of fir decking, supported by a log column at the far left. ABOVE: The dining space in the cottage, flanked by a log column in the foreground.

Mark and Bonnie wanted to build a cottage on a wooded plot of land they had purchased on the western shore of Madeline Island. From the building site, one can gaze across the broad, cold waters of Lake Superior. At night, the twinkling lights of Bayfield beckon on the opposite shore. Their goals for the cottage were to provide a peaceful, comfortable respite from their busy everyday lives in Duluth, where Mark is a physician and Bonnie a nurse anesthetist. The cottage was to be of an intimate scale, with rooms in which they and their two growing children, Aaron and Emily, could be together and connect as a family on weekends throughout the year. They hoped the cottage would have the welcoming, magical, come-hither feeling of Lundie's cabins on the North Shore.

I designed and detailed the cottage with the assistance of two long term colleagues, architect Maury Stenerson and Jessica Wilder. We sited the building so that it peers through a screen of trees to the water. The tree screen provided literal and psychological protection from the immense lake and the prevailing northwest winds. Two future pieces of construction, a sauna and a garage with a sleeping loft above it, were linked in a circle by a walking path within close range of the cottage. The three linked pieces create the sense of a small community.

The form of the cabin itself was broken into three pieces, three gabled forms with steeply pitched roofs that telescope out from one another, diminishing in size as they proceed. This arrangement allowed for lake-facing windows in both sides of the corners of the rooms in the forms, doubling the size and angle of the lake views. As well, they provided light from two sides, a Pattern Language concept that I have used frequently.

BELOW: *Viewed from the kitchen, a comfortable grouping of upholstered furniture pieces surround the Chilton stone fireplace. The lakeside screened porch is accessed by a French door to the left of the fireplace.*

RIGHT: *The carved fir newel post and vertical railing balusters of the stairway.* FACING: *A fireplace in the screened porch extends the use of the porch from spring through fall.*

The floor plans on both the main and upper levels of the cottage reflect the same jogs. On the second floor, a trio of shed dormers lifts up from the steep roofs, with windows that gaze towards the lake.

A massive post carved from a single timber welcomes the visitor to the entry, nestled in an alcove under the big gabled roof. Overhead is a trellis that seems to grow out of the post. One enters through an extra wide wood door with an arched rounded top.

On the main level, living, dining, and cooking activities are contained within a single room, which one enters through that wide arched door. The room is built using the post-and-beam method of construction. Another big carved log column, the mate of the one guarding the entry, stands at the corner of the kitchen, supporting a lowered wood ceiling over that space. Here, the massive log posts extend the welcoming presence of the cottage to its interior: pieces of the architectural structure in the room relate to the scale of the human body. (My partner Dale Mulfinger is fond of saying that he likes to put big wood columns in a space so that when you come in it feels like somebody is already home.) Deep wood beams of Douglas fir support exposed wood decking on the ceilings above, and the walls are wrapped with tongue-and-groove pine boards.

The room is anchored by a huge stone hearth in the corner, which accommodates a Rumford masonry fireplace in the living room, and another fireplace around the corner in the adjacent screened porch. The raised sitting hearth sweeps around to form the first step of the stair next to it. On the other side of the stone hearth mass is another fireplace, located in the screened porch that wraps around

the lakeside corner of the house. The fireplace wards off the chill in late spring and early fall evenings. The flickering light from its flames illuminates carefully laid stone walls.

In an alcove off the kitchen is a bright sunlit window seat, offering a cozy spot to read or reflect. The seat was designed to be away from the main gathering space around the hearth but within earshot of the activity there. Down a short hallway beyond is a secluded main bedroom suite, which occupies the space within the smallest gabled form at the end of the house. It enjoys light and views from three sides and feels almost like a little house itself within the cottage.

At the stone landing, stairs rise along a winding path toward the second level. They are graced by hand-carved newel posts and railings, which resemble the large carved columns at a smaller scale. The upper portion of the stair is a tiny bridge across open space, supported by shaped structural brackets below it. The second floor contains two bedrooms and a shared bathroom. They are contained in the

ABOVE: A ship's ladder leads from the second floor to a hideaway loft in the uppermost peak of the roof. To the right is a shared study open to the entry below. FACING: A sunlit window seat in an alcove adjoining the kitchen and the living room.

LEFT: *Thick fir brackets support a staircase landing at the second floor.* RIGHT: *In the main bedroom, a pine shelf supported by brackets surrounds the head of the bed. Small windows above the shelf bring the morning light into the room. An additional small window just below the shelf offers a lake breeze and a pillowside glimpse of the woods beyond.*

volume of the three steeply pitched roof gables, and they offer glimpses of the lake through a series of shed dormers that emerge from the steeply pitched roofs. Built-in beds are tucked under the low portion of the slanting rooflines.

From the second-floor hallway, a ship's ladder offers access to a loft space in the very peak of the highest roof. Strewn with sleeping bags and beanbag chairs, the room lies within the embrace of its steeply angled side walls, and a small window at the end wall provides a view over the treetops to the lake.

The Madeline Island cottage is highly detailed and ornamental in every aspect. At the entry a panel of ceramic tiles, custom painted by local artist De De Eckels, celebrates Native American themes and symbols: intertwined symmetrical stem-like shapes interspersed with animal and human forms. At the stair landing, a stained glass window depicts stylized oak leaves emanating from a central stem, a similarly natural theme rendered in a different medium.

Above all, the cottage is a rich example of the use of structure as ornament. The massive, carved log posts were carefully wrought by builders William (Tibbs) Tibble and Mike North. The wood columns invite the touch of the hand as one passes by. They seem like strong, cheerful, trustworthy fellows, content in their role of supporting the deep fir beams and the floor above.

The theme of hand-carved wood members is repeated at various levels of scale throughout the house. Chunky carved posts support the table-like island. The newel posts at the stair are similarly detailed, with rhythmic concentric indentations, as

LEFT: *The screen on the sauna porch is embellished with flowing leaf-like shapes.* BELOW: *The sauna building, viewed from the lake-facing porch of the cottage.*

are the smaller vertical railing members. Supportive brackets, both inside and out, are carefully shaped. These elements are simultaneously structural and ornamental. They do structural work, as well as delight the eye.

One senses the structural strength of their emphatic arched gesture, as well as the fact that their contoured forms are clearly made by hand. The structural timber pieces, columns, beams, and outriggers remind us of the careful attention and skill of the craftsmen who formed them.

A wood screen surrounding the outdoor shower stall at the sauna building is a particularly evocative example of combined function and beauty. The lead carpenter, Matt Scheider, cut a flowing pattern of leaf-like shapes out of adjacent 1 by 4 cedar boards, each of which is separated from its neighbor by a ¾-inch open space. Light passing through the varied openings creates a secondary image of the graceful pattern, which Scheider says reminded him of the waves on the lake. The result is whimsical, beautiful, and functional all at once.

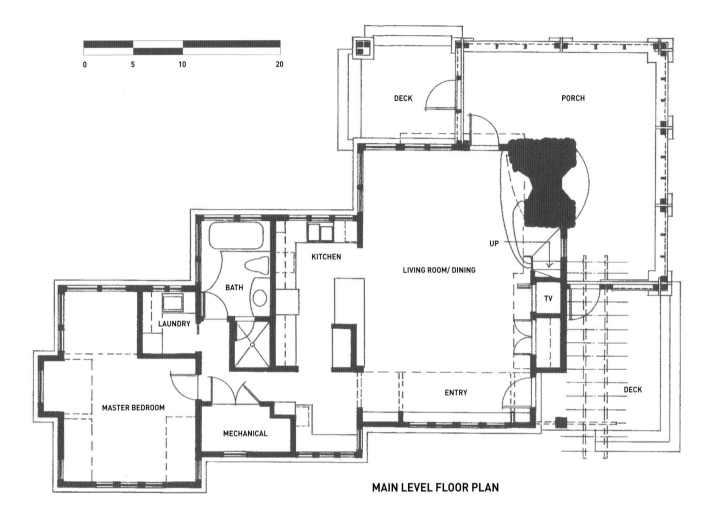

DECK

PORCH

KITCHEN

LIVING ROOM/ DINING

UP

BATH

TV

LAUNDRY

ENTRY

DECK

MASTER BEDROOM

MECHANICAL

0   5   10   20

MAIN LEVEL FLOOR PLAN

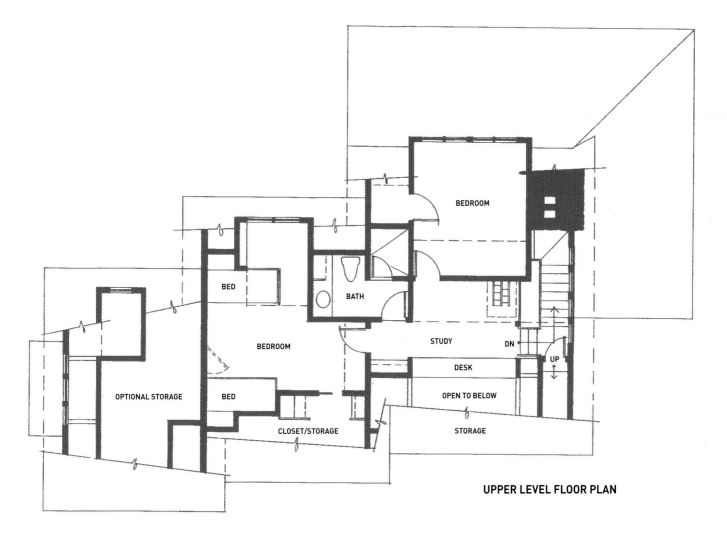

BEDROOM

BED

BATH

BEDROOM

STUDY

DN

UP

DESK

OPTIONAL STORAGE

BED

OPEN TO BELOW

CLOSET/STORAGE

STORAGE

UPPER LEVEL FLOOR PLAN

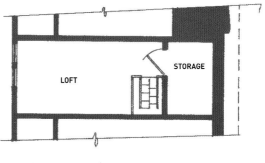

LOFT

STORAGE

3RD LEVEL LOFT

MELDING WORK AND HOME

IT IS A PLEASANT PARADOX that as we observe the ever widening reach of global communication, we can reap the benefit, if we choose, of living our lives in a more contained, smaller sphere. More and more of us, pressed for time, faced with the needs of growing families and aging parents, and increasingly aware of both personal and global energy consumption, elect to dump our commutes and pursue our work lives close to home.

The space necessary for working at home can be an alcove carved out of a room in one's home, the conversion of an underused space to one tailored to a specific activity, or the addition of new space to work in, either connected to or detached from the home.

Communities and the planning commissions that represent them are becoming increasingly aware of the ways in which cottage industry can enrich and strengthen the substance of community life. Rather than being forced to choose between work and home life, we can decide to choose both. Instead of leaving and returning to homes that stand empty most of the day, people can choose to work at home, still connected to the workplace, and better connected to their family members and neighbors. Children can understand and acknowledge the work of a parent as a necessary part of daily life, while benefiting from having that parent much more present in their lives. New links between people are forged by daily interactions, and the community itself becomes a stronger, more vital place.

A good example of such progressive policies occurs in the town where my family and I live, Stillwater, Minnesota. Here, one can build an "accessory dwelling unit"

on a lot that is a minimum of 10,000 square feet. The accessory building can be used for living space, as a rentable apartment, quarters for a nanny, or a caretaker for the elderly. One can also obtain a conditional use permit and use the space for a workplace, with certain restrictions that emphasize not disturbing the community by the work performed in it. This ordinance represents an enlightened new attitude in Stillwater toward city planning and use of local resources. It embraces the notion of potentially increasing density in order to increase the presence of people actually in the community during the day. It also increases the versatility and number of years a home can be suitable for a particular family, with resultant greater pride in that extended ownership. Current land and water resources are used, rather than developing more land and introducing more homes and infrastructure to create more habitable space. Also, within the historic districts of Stillwater, homeowners are eligible to receive property tax discounts for historically sensitive additions to existing properties.

Our family moved to Stillwater from nearby Minneapolis in 1995. By 1997, SALA Architects, the firm in which I am a partner, established a branch office exactly one mile from our home. There went one commute! Still, my husband drove fifty minutes each way daily to our glass studio, Pegasus Studio Inc., in Minneapolis. We perused the existing stock of available rental space in Stillwater but were discouraged to find that the rent was twice as expensive as our storefront space in Minneapolis. That brought us to the happy realization that it would actually be more cost effective to build a space for our studio on our own property, thus realizing a dream we'd had for many years. By building the studio in 2000, we were able to have more time to spend with our daughter and each other, and more time to do our work. Looking back on it, my only regret is that we didn't do it sooner.

When we initially purchased our home, a gracious old Craftsman foursquare, we noticed that the garage roof leaked. In fact, it had leaked for years; water infiltration had rotted all the rafters and large portions of the walls. When pieces of the roof began to fall on our vehicles, we finally found it completely unusable. So we decided to combine the new studio space with the garage and solve both problems at once. I set about designing a spacious carriage house. The lower level of the carriage house would accommodate our "carriages," a Mini Cooper and an ancient Volvo station wagon. The upper level would house our art glass studio.

Working at home and actually managing to accomplish something while working meant for us that the workplace needed to be separate rather than attached to the dwelling. We felt that some degree of physical separation and psychological separation from the ongoing work was necessary. The nature of glasswork requires such a separation—trotting over tiny glass shards on the way to the bathroom is not appealing. And though having the studio so close was a great convenience, it seemed right to be able to leave it at the end of the day and still be able to "go home."

The typical pattern of building in our historic neighborhood was of a detached building (a garage, a carriage house, or small storage cottage) positioned at the rear of a site. So the carriage house took shape as a simple rectangular form, one and a

half stories tall. It was located towards the rear of the lot, in roughly the same spot that the previous garage had occupied, accessible from the street by the existing driveway on the south side of the property. Because it was an accessory dwelling unit, which could potentially serve as an apartment, the setbacks were somewhat bigger than the setbacks for the previous detached garage: 7 feet 6 inches from the side yard lot line, and 25 feet from the rear lot line. This pushed the footprint of the carriage house forward toward the home, shortening our walk with groceries into the house by about 20 feet. But it still left a distance of some 15 feet between the two buildings, enough to establish a sense of threshold between the driveway area and the garden.

The carriage house building became a little sister of sorts to the main house. I used the same roof pitch, 6/12, but in order that the building not appear too tall from the street, the eaves of the roof were brought way down on the entry side, and the peak of the roof occurs about nearly three-fourths of the way down the length of the building, instead of in the center of the building, as it does on the traditional

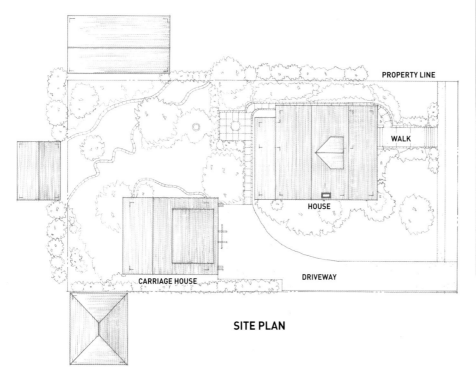

PROPERTY LINE

WALK

HOUSE

CARRIAGE HOUSE

DRIVEWAY

SITE PLAN

Though having the studio so close was a great convenience,
it seemed RIGHT to be able TO LEAVE IT at the end of the day
and still be able to "go home."

The carriage house is about 15 feet from the back porch of the house, and the garden to the right adjoins both buildings. With the windows open in temperate weather, we can chat back and forth between the two buildings.

Craftsman house. This established a sort of kinship between the two pieces, without repeating precisely the same form.

The carriage house was built by Dave Wallin and Joe Anderson of Anderson Wallin Construction. The structure is a fairly simple form, but it is attired in full Craftsman dress, that is, lots of exterior details, which Dave and Joe crafted with great care. Emulating the main house, the carriage house roof has deep sheltering eaves supported by sturdy timber brackets, broad fascia and trim, and wood double-hung windows. It is clad in narrow clapboard siding of cedar, beautifully mitered at the corners. The two broad gable ends are covered in sawn shingles, and at either side a slightly cantilevered extension pops out on the upper level, creating a bit more space in the studio above, and adding definition to the long sides of the building that face our yard and the neighboring yard.

The two garage doors were created by adding small windows in the upper panels of standard insulated garage doors. Siding and trim were then applied to the face of the doors, to suggest the appearance of the vertical panels characteristic of doors on traditional outbuildings. The garage doors are located on either side of a central "person" door, which is accented by a trellis overhead.

The colors of the carriage house echo those of the main house: a vivid terracotta color on the horizontal siding, grayish green on the sawn shingles, windows, and window boxes, doors of a deep purple, and a soft creamy yellow on the trim, trellis, and fascia, binding together the whole composition.

Our backyard space is bordered on all four sides by adjacent buildings: a neighbor's garage, a neighbor's workspace in a building once used as a stable, our own home, and the long side of our carriage house. This space in between our work and our home became semi-enclosed garden space: a sheltered, private outdoor room, partly enclosed by the walls of the adjacent buildings, screened by plantings, with a leafy ceiling provided by the tree canopy.

The sense of enclosure is heightened in a patio walled by arborvitae trees, which creates a room within a room. It is a smaller, more intimate space within the outdoor garden room. The patio is furnished with a table and chairs for outdoor dining. An arched doorway of tree branches creates a passage between the two areas.

Upstairs in the studio, windows receive light from all four directions, an important factor in selecting glass for windows in specific light exposures. Large simple work surfaces are filled with ongoing glass projects for public spaces, residences, and churches. Though the studio is relatively small in terms of size (750 square feet), we are capable of producing very large projects in it. Most glass installations are composed of a series of individual panels that range in size from four to sixteen square feet each. These are stored during the fabrication process on racks filled with horizontal trays, which are tucked into the lower portions of the roof volume. They contain portions of windows for which the glass is already cut, prior to glazing assembly.

The sense of enclosure is heightened in a patio walled by arborvitae trees, which creates A ROOM WITHIN A ROOM. It is a smaller, more intimate space within the outdoor garden room.

LEFT: *Two Siamese*
sentinels watch over the garden.
The more suspicious of the two
is ever mindful of the birdbaths.

ABOVE: *Walls of arborvitae*
trees screen a patio for alfresco
dining. An arched opening frames
a view of the garden beyond

We draw large-scale murals in the studio for etched and carved glass artwork. Sculptural pieces of glass, stone, and metal are designed in the studio and partially fabricated there. The metal and stone elements are fabricated by other craftspeople, and the entire piece is then assembled and installed on the actual site.

My particular workspace is a long table that overlooks the garden space below. While I design windows or draw the figures for projects of carved and etched glass, or work on clay projects to be cast in bronze, my husband, John Pietras, is busy cutting the glass, assembling, and soldering the panels at the other work areas.

The studio is simply one of my most favorite places to be. When John and I are there together, the rhythm of our separate activities carries us through the day, interspersed by comfortable bits of conversation. I can envision the space in the future serving as a small apartment for the two of us, while the main house could be rented. The space could house a caregiver, or a nanny for future owners. Its separation from the house and the garden space in between offers many possibilities for future use. Each structure provides privacy for dwelling and activity, while the shared yard offers opportunities for relaxation and connection.

COLOR, LANDSCAPE, AND DWELLING

✧ OUR EXPERIENCE OF COLOR is an ephemeral dance with our experience of light. Each night, color leaves us and returns again in the morning with the rising sun. We sense color by means of rods and cones in our eyes, which are not sensitive enough to register color at low levels of light. Thus we see only shades of gray and black in moonlight. As light is reduced even further, we are increasingly unable to decipher even basic forms. But in the morning, the rays of the sun reveal a world of color, form, and texture to us once more.

The light and color we perceive in our natural environment changes throughout the day, as the angle of the sun varies during the course of each day, and throughout the seasons. In northern climes, the summer sun brings a surfeit of light and color. The meager, hesitant light of winter reveals a very different place, colored in cool tones of white and pale grays and blues, dusty shades of brown and black, with shadows of vibrant deep blue, black, and purple. The changing colors of nature throughout the course of a year are a continuing inspiration for local artists, such as Morgan Clifford. Clifford recently explored the moods and colors of winter in a woven tapestry of linen, silk, hemp, paper, aloo, and cotton (above).

The subdued palette of winter and its fleeting crystalline light are qualities that have long been themes of the glasswork that my husband, John Pietras, and I produce at Pegasus Studio.

Color comes from nature, from culture, and from history. Our experience of the light and color in our own natural landscape and environment deeply influences the way we think about color and the way we use it in our daily lives. This phenomenon

The harborside piazza in Vernazza, Italy, is ringed with tall building facades in various shades of stucco: coral, rose, burgundy, cream, gold, and olive. The stone base of the church merges with the deep gray waterside cliffs. PREVIOUS PAGE:

A screen of leaded glass separates two adjacent spaces at the Indigo Building in Red Wing, Minnesota. Hand-blown glass of blue and gray, clear textured glass and carved bevels evoke the crystalline qualities of a winter landscape. By Pegasus Studio.

is perhaps most apparent when we step out of our everyday environment and experience another place, climate, and culture. For the last ten years or so, our family has traveled to Italy every summer. We have particularly enjoyed the town of Vernazza, in the Cinque Terre region on the Ligurian coast. There, as in many Mediterranean hillside towns, colorful stucco and stone buildings are stacked side by side. As they spring up from the rocky landscape, their forms merge together, forming an organic yet ordered jumble of color and texture. The steep hillsides around the town are cultivated with vineyards, which cling to the rocky soil. They are contained by laboriously constructed stone ledges encircling the mountain slopes in rhythmic lines. Casual sheds and small work cottages are strewn throughout the vineyards, providing a spot of shade and place of respite during the workday.

Vernazza is a one-street town. Its main street lies at the bottom of the cleft between two steep cliffs. Buildings are built into the sides of the cliffs as they ascend in either direction. The houses on the hillsides are accessed by steep steps on winding paths that are literally carved out of the rock. Buildings farther from the center of town, and those located on the rocky hillsides leading to Corniglia and Monterosso, are more likely to be composed of brick or stone. The colors of these building materials—grays, browns, creamy golds and tans—come directly from the native stone and soil. The main street proceeds down to the water; the buildings lining it are built of the same stone or brick masonry, with colorful overcoats of stucco. A few even boast faded frescoed borders. Main Street culminates at the harborside Piazza Marconi, which is the living room of the entire town. The buildings that ring the piazza are adjoining facades. They display a wide array of hues: ochre, grayish green, terra cotta, amber, vanilla, burnt sienna, deep oxblood red, and various shades of rose, salmon, and pink. Fragments of the striated greenish gray local stone emerge from the stucco at portals and thresholds. Ubiquitous green shutters strike a common note in the overall composition, shading the interior rooms during the hot sunny days and opening to the sea breezes in the evenings. The colors of the facades distinguish one from the next. They form a pleasingly coherent whole of disparate but proudly independent pieces. They are joined together but simultaneously distinct and individual, like the members of a family.

The stucco buildings are built over brick, stone, or concrete walls. Their colors reflect human choices and personal expression. They are also defined by local custom and historical tradition. The structures tend to contrast with the surrounding summer greenery. Sometimes the colors derive from the natural tones of earth and foliage (rust, terra-cotta, ochre, and green). In other instances the colors are drawn from more vivid examples of natural colors, such as the varied hues of flowering plants (roses, bougainvillea, multihued hydrangeas, the brilliant yellow of the agave

blossoms), fruits, and vegetables (eggplants, currants, grapes, raspberries, tomatoes, lemons, and limes).

Experiencing other environments and cultures gives us the opportunity to widen our personal palettes. It also, by virtue of contrast, gives us the tools to understand how our own surroundings and culture influence our color preferences. The use of color on buildings, especially houses, may be seen as related to an overall attitude towards the site. Charles Moore's theory that buildings can either merge with or lay claim to the land around them can be further extended to the use of color. The colors of a building can be purposefully chosen to heighten the way in which a building merges or blends with its site. Or they can be chosen in a way that heightens how a building lays claim to its site, by the use of tones that contrast with the colors in the landscape.

My brother Mark Mahady and his wife, Therese, and son, Adam, asked me to design a house for them in Carmel Valley, California. It is a house that merges with its site, both in form and color.

ABOVE: *The trellis provides a shaded spot on the deck of ipe wood.* FACING: *Under the trellis: outdoor dining with shade and a view.*

The house, which I designed with architect Maury Stenerson, is built on the side of a southwest-facing hill. It has expansive views both up the hill to the north and down the hill to the east, south, and west. The hills in that area of California near Big Sur suggest furry patient beasts, with velvety rounded paws that stretch out towards the flat land around them. In the winter and early spring, the hillsides are covered in varying shades of green. As the rainfall decreases during the summer, the grasses gradually change into tones of light gold, taupe, dusty brown, and beige. Tree foliage on the hills remains green and contrasts with the predominant neutral tones of the grasses. The color of the soil itself around the house is a light dusty tan, with natural shale of light gold, cream, and gray. While siting the house, we found numerous tiny fossils embedded in the loose shale, and we based the coloration of the house on the colors found in the shale and fossilized rocks.

Mark and Therese's home is composed of long, low-slung forms, with shallowly pitched and flat roofs. Its form is partially built into the hill behind it, and the

The COLORS AND FORMS REINFORCE one
another to create a sense of a strong bond between the house and the land.

rooflines stretch out horizontally from the hillside, almost suggesting that it is the land itself extending out.

Therese and I studied the colors of the land carefully. We used the pieces of rock and soil we had gathered to guide us in making color choices that would heighten the effect of the house being an extension of the land. The exterior walls are two shades of stucco, light tan and taupe.

The windows are a light pebble gray, and the wood trim around them is painted a light cocoa color, slightly darker than the stucco. The asphalt shingles on the sloped roofs is a subtle tan and gray mix, and the gravel on the flat roofs is a light brown. On the sunny southwest side of the house, a spacious deck of ipe wood flows around the house, shaded by an extensive trellis of Douglas fir. Both have been allowed to naturally weather to a fine, silvery gray.

The sloped soffits below the eaves descend directly into the ceilings of the open living and kitchen area. The ceilings are painted a shade just a bit deeper than that of the walls, to bring them down a bit in scale visually so that they don't feel uncomfortably high.

A lower ceiling extends over the kitchen island area, to bring a sense of intimacy and shelter to that spot. The floors are of warm cherrywood. The cabinetry and millwork is of maple, and the countertops are of creamy golden travertine marble. The fireplace mass within the house is built of grayish gold native Carmel stone, to which we added some of the tiny fossils that Adam found during construction.

The combined effect of the carefully chosen colors is a subtle palette of light, shade, and color drawn directly from the landscape. The colors and forms reinforce one another to create a sense of a strong bond between the house and the land. The house seems to literally emerge from the earth around it.

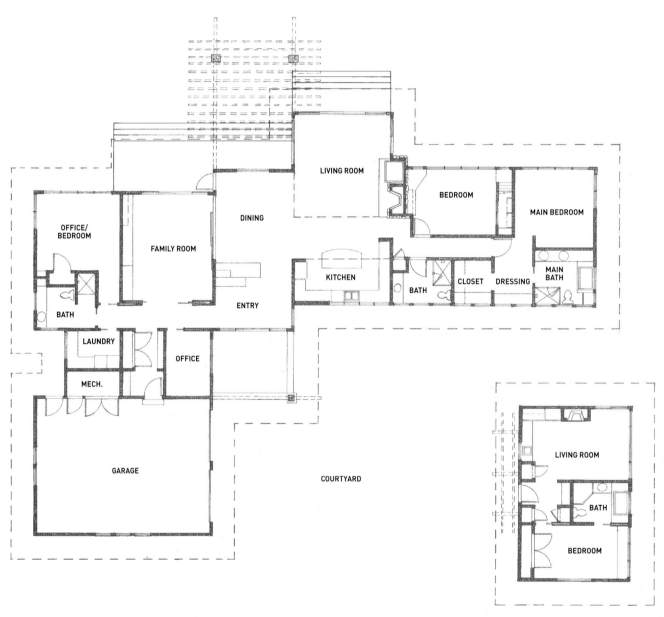

OFFICE/
BEDROOM

FAMILY ROOM

LIVING ROOM

DINING

BEDROOM

MAIN BEDROOM

BATH

KITCHEN

ENTRY

BATH

CLOSET

DRESSING

MAIN
BATH

LAUNDRY

OFFICE

MECH.

GARAGE

COURTYARD

FLOOR PLAN

LIVING ROOM

BATH

BEDROOM

GUEST HOUSE

ABOVE: *The interior of the home is an open flowing space defined by varying ceiling heights. The floors are American cherry wood, and the millwork is maple. In the sun-filled rooms, the colors of the walls are slightly lighter than the ceilings.*

RIGHT: *The fireplace is of native Carmel stone. It is flanked by a cherry cabinet with a deep alcove above it.*

FACING: *The dusky green color of the foyer alcove is a pleasing contrast to the golden shade of the stairwell beyond.* ABOVE: *The simple lines of the house echo agrarian buildings of the region.*

A cottage home here in Stillwater, Minnesota, pays homage to its site and to its owners by the expressive and personal way color is used in it.

A few years ago Jeff and Heather purchased a double lot on the North Hill in Stillwater. A barn had originally stood on the southeastern portion of the land, but it was no longer in existence. Their intention was to live in the house on the northwestern side of the site, while building a compact, economical home on the open land to the southeast. It was to be a home for them and their two young daughters, Elli and Maci. They emphasized their desire for quality versus quantity in the home. They wanted the house to be a good fit with the neighboring houses and to have minimal impact on the feeling of the established community. They hoped the house would feel like it had been there a long time.

They discussed these goals with architects Dale Mulfinger and Debra Kees of SALA. Dale and Deb produced a series of schematic sketches of a comfortable cozy house, with simple strong forms rooted in the agrarian buildings of the Midwest countryside.

The home is designed in 4′ 0″ increments to easily facilitate the economy of panelized construction. It featured low maintenance cementitious siding in a vertical board-and-batten pattern. The fenestration is simple and bold: white doublehung window units with minimal trim. Honoring the original barn on the site (and because it's Heather's favorite color), the house was to be painted red. A few exterior walls are accented in a shade of mossy green.

The front door opens off a welcoming front porch that wraps around the corner of the building. The front doorway enters a small foyer space, an alcove beside the stair, which contains a low storage chest strewn with pillows. It's a spot for visitors

Heather uses slightly deeper shades
of a closely **RELATED COLOR** on distant outer
walls to give the space a sense of shadow and depth.

➾ABOVE: *The island, clad in painted beadwood, feels like a partition wall and gracefully separates the living room from the kitchen area.* RIGHT: *The*

main living/dining/kitchen space is painted with slightly varying shades of soft green. A beamed ceiling overhead unifies and delineates the room.

The sink area is screened from view by a broad wood plank ledge located slightly above the work surface of the island.

to sit while pulling off and stowing their boots. The stairwell to the left is colored a warm sunny gold, providing a delightful contrasting interplay with the white wood handrail and the adjacent foyer walls of grayish green.

To the right of the entry is an L-shaped open room that contains dining, kitchen, and living areas. Its nine-foot-high ceiling is defined by cedar beams, with areas of lower soffitted ceilings against the walls to provide a feeling of shelter around particular activities. The warm glow of resawn pine plank floors connects the spaces. The walls throughout are of closely varying shades of soft green. Heather uses slightly deeper shades of a closely related color on distant outer walls to give the space a sense of shadow and depth. Adjoining the main room is a diminutive study/ sitting/reading room. A desk and computer are tucked into a corner just out of view, and a couple of comfy chairs on the other side of the room offer a fine spot to read or have a quiet chat. The room is painted a dusky shade of violet, reflecting the contemplative nature of the activities that take place in it. The kitchen is on the sunny south side of the house. Painted white kitchen cabinetry with the character of cottage furniture lines the western wall.

The Swansons' home takes advantage of the everyday family connections afforded by the open kitchen/dining/living arrangement. But often these kinds of spaces can feel as if the casual working kitchen is an ungainly imposition jammed into the space. Here the architects deftly worked with lowered ceiling thresholds between adjacent areas to define spaces within the whole. Also, the kitchen area is "de-kitchenized" by the use of distinctive furniture-like cabinetry. The commodious center island across from the bank of cabinets is built in a manner that belies its everyday function. The side that faces the living room is clad with pine beadboard siding painted a deep warm red. From the living room opposite, the island feels like an interior partition wall rather than an extension of the kitchen.

The family enters from the two-stall garage on the east side of the house into a cheerful, practical, and durable room floored with contrasting checks of deep red and white linoleum. The space is within easy reach of an alcove for laundry, and it's a short jaunt from the garage to the kitchen with bags of groceries.

The sunny golden stairwell and the hallway above are illuminated by a set of small square east-facing windows situated high on the wall near the sloping ceiling. "The golden color and the light pull you through the house," Heather says, and Jeff adds, "When you are dragging yourself out of bed on a winter morning, it's a cheerful sight." Three bedrooms and two baths are nestled with the volumes of the pitched roof, so that the side walls are low knee walls and the ceilings slope up from them. Jeff and Heather's bedroom is painted a serene shade between green and blue, called "water green."

Coming into the project, both Heather and Jeff were well versed in the way a house can express itself through form, texture, and color. They speak highly of the role that their architects Mulfinger and Kees played in designing the house. Deb Kees described that role, saying, "Here the architect was an aide to the owners, working to help them translate and create their own vision."

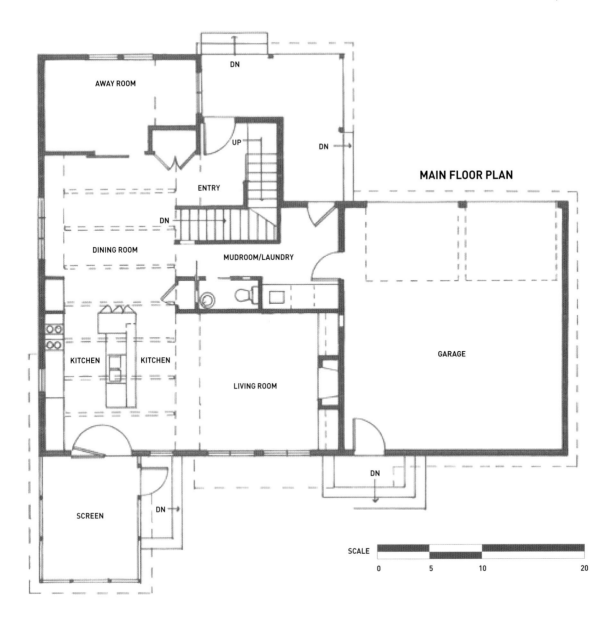

MAIN FLOOR PLAN

AWAY ROOM

DN

UP

DN

ENTRY

DN

DINING ROOM

MUDROOM/LAUNDRY

GARAGE

KITCHEN   KITCHEN

LIVING ROOM

SCREEN

DN

DN

SCALE

0	5	10	20

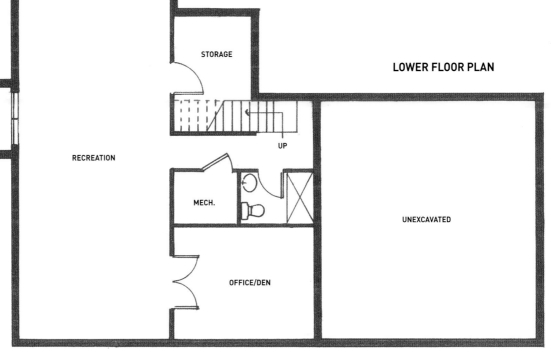

STORAGE

LOWER FLOOR PLAN

RECREATION

UP

MECH.

UNEXCAVATED

OFFICE/DEN

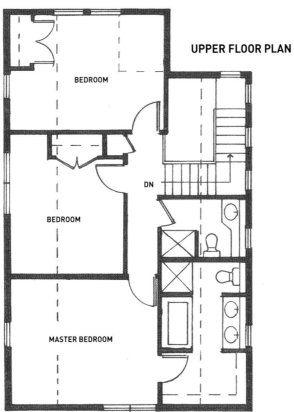

UPPER FLOOR PLAN

BEDROOM

DN

BEDROOM

MASTER BEDROOM

THE RIGHT FIT TO THE EARTH

AT SALA ARCHITECTS, our firm in Minnesota, we have long focused on creating homes that are energy-efficient, enduring structures. They are artfully crafted, of materials native to the region, designed and built to lie lightly on the land. We have long supported the notion of building less rather than more, emphasizing the qualitative aspects of space rather than quantitative ones. These attitudes have resulted in well-insulated, smaller homes that exhibit very modest energy consumption and a low carbon footprint. As Dan Chiras points out in his book *The Solar House*, "Building smaller dwellings reduces the resources that must be marshaled to create and maintain shelter. Smaller homes mean less clear cutting, less mining, less paint, and less fossil fuel energy for making building materials and maintaining comfort. Smaller size also slashes construction costs and reduces the amount of land that must be disturbed to create human shelter."

Careful attention to the relationship of a house to its site is key to developing the means by which a home can become a sensitive and responsible part of the environment. Thoughtful orientation of the house to the path of the sun, using landscape elements and the earth itself to create shelter from the wind, positioning of openings to maximize the potential for solar heating and cooling, and introducing thermal mass throughout the home, which absorbs heat during the day and releases it slowly during the night, are among the techniques that Chiras suggests.

In the summer of 2005, I received an email from Brad Bruno and Toni Schaeffer, an idealistic young couple with great reverence for the environment. They wanted to build what they called "a passive-aggressive" solar house on their sunny,

expansive site in the Schoharie Valley of New York, near Schenectady. It was to be a house that would honor both the land and the sun, an energy-efficient passive solar house that could also incorporate future active solar elements and yet, as they put it, "not look like a new-age spaceship."

We first visited the site together on a sultry day in August. The land, about 15 acres in size, was one of those sweeping, vista filled places that makes you draw in your breath at the very first sight of it. And it was an absolutely ideal spot for building a passive solar house: a south facing hill, with unobstructed distant southern views of the Helderberg Mountains, a small mountain range that connects with the foothills of the Catskills. Sheltering groves of trees surrounded the building site to the west, east, and north. There were several spots on the land that would have been suitable for the house, and we discussed the pros and cons of each before settling on building at the crest of the hill. This placement was nearest the shelter of the trees that ringed the west, north and east sides, closest to the road, and provided the most extensive views of the rolling site, a pond that they envisioned building in the mid distance, a neighboring farm, gentle grassy foothills beyond that, and the rounded, bluish-purple forms of the mountains beyond them.

The ideal form for phase one of construction was a simple rectangle, with the long east-west axis within 10 degrees east or west of true south, so that the house could gain as much sunlight as possible.

We also discussed solar design guidelines, which Brad and Toni had compiled from a variety of sources. They included rules of thumb such as the following:

1. The building should be relatively long and narrow, with the long axis aligned east to west.

2. 10–13 percent of the square footage should be south-facing glass.

3. Be careful of east- or west-facing glass; this can lead to overheating. Any west-facing windows will require some form of summer shading.

4. Limit north-facing glass, which can cause heat loss in the winter.

5. Open floor plans work best for heat distribution. Try to work with plans that are only one room deep. Place circulation and service areas at the north side of the plan.

6. For every square foot of south glass, use 150 pounds of masonry or 4 gallons of water for thermal mass.

7. Use thermal mass at less thickness throughout the living space (such as a floor slab), rather than a concentrated area of thicker mass. Do not cover thermal mass floors with wall-to-wall carpeting; keep as bare as functionally and aesthetically possible. The surface area of mass exposed to direct sunlight should be 6–9 times the area of the glazing.

8. Open floor plans make the best use of thermal mass. Thermal mass swings should be at most 10 degrees Fahrenheit.

9. Use a medium dark color for masonry floors; use light colors for other lightweight walls; thermal mass walls can be any color.

10. Limit solar gain collection area such that average inside temperature is no greater than 72 degrees on a sunny January day. A heat load analysis of the house should be

⇌ The windows of the southern facade welcome the sun.

conducted. (This would require a computer simulation with Energy 10 software.)

11. Insulate foundations, floors, ceilings, and walls.

12. Regulate the amount of sun that enters the house by means of overhangs and shading.

With Brad and Toni's ideas, pictures of the site, and these Twelve Commandments of Passive Solar Design in hand, I was ready to start designing. I started with the long rectangular plan form suggested and followed the patterns of Toni and Brad's daily activities to locate rooms on the sunny side. Rather than running the ridge of the roof along the long east-west axis, with small roof gables at either end, I turned to a precedent I'd often seen in New England. This form is a long, narrow house, with the roof ridge spanning the short distance at the center, going from north to south.

This provided a large gabled face to the south, where the major expanse of windows would be. It also provided a canvas for the friendly welcoming face on the entry side of the house, to the driveway area on the north side of the house. A smaller version of the same form housed the service areas on the main floor (laundry, mud room, mechanical, pantry, and a half bath). A long leg of this secondary roof sheltered an inviting entry porch. Garage space was to be provided in a future pole barn near the north side of the house. A gently curving path led from the barn to the front porch entry.

The second-level floor was framed with exposed beams, purlins, and decking to provide the sheltering, woven wood feeling that Toni had sought for the ceiling of the main level. The two bedrooms and bath all open off a central landing of about 8 × 10 feet in size, which serves double duty as a secluded study/office space. Under the lower edges of the SIPS roof on the east and west ends, spaces were left open to below, with shuttered interior windows in the bedrooms above to provide for heat circulation to the second floor.

Brad analyzed the house design on his Energy 10 software. The goal was to have a "net zero energy house." This means that (averaged over time) all of the energy needs of the house would be met passively or generated renewably. He was able to simulate the heat gain conditions for the house as designed, with the window locations and size shown, the SIPS, the broad overhangs, the seasonal awnings, a hot water radiant floor slab, and the central thermal mass. He studied the effect of slightly varying angles to true south to see if there was any combination of better energy efficiency with more favorable views. Brad's analysis suggested a good deal less glazing on the west side and more summer shading on that side too. Architect Meghan Cornell of SALA created section drawings of the interior spaces, carefully assembling the house plans with an eye to the 4-foot modules of the SIPS panels. She also drew and detailed the post-and-beam structure within the SIPS shell and the substantial bracket and porch outside. We cut down the square footage of glazing on the west side by changing the windows into small, high transom units, and also reduced the size of the north and east facing windows to very small punched

ABOVE LEFT: *Warm red windows and roofing are complemented by neutral tones of brown, tan, and gray drawn from the native stone obtained from the site.* ABOVE RIGHT: *Long horizontal view of the site and the house.*

⤳ *Broad bands of south-facing windows create a glowing, welcoming entry.*

thermal energy collectors would most likely be necessary to meet the zero net energy goals. A whole house heat exchanger for make-up air was also planned for.

Construction began about a year and a half later, overseen by general contractor Ethan Eberly of Best Built Construction, Oneonta, New York. Stonework at the low walls and the interior central stone mass were sensitively crafted by Ward Hamilton of Olde Mohawk Masonry, Nisskayuna, New York. The new stonework is an enduring and beautiful complement to the old dry stacked walls that existed on the site.

Despite its focus on energy efficiency, the house is definitely not reminiscent of a new age spaceship. It's a small, tidy, welcoming cottage. It is at home on the land it sprang from and is warmed naturally by the sun. As Toni reports, "It seems like it was always there."

⤳

In January 2007, architect Bryan Anderson of the SALA office in Minneapolis was contacted by Jeff and Shelly Zierdt. They had purchased a home on a 3 1/2–acre piece of land on the shore of the Mississippi River near Monticello, Minnesota. The house, built through the winter of 2007–2008, was on a bluff only eighty eight feet from the river. Its windows faced north to a spectacular view over the water below.

The qualities of the land, the light, and the water spoke to the Zierdts immediately and strongly. However, the qualities of the house itself did not. Its layout was dysfunctional and confusing. It was precariously perched too close to the bluff. The exterior form of the house and plan inside it had been altered by a series of clumsy additions. Nevertheless, they were eager to move from their previous home in central Wisconsin, so they moved into the house despite its shortcomings. They made a few changes to better the house, but they realized that these efforts were not a long-term cure for the bigger problems the house had. They were perplexed as to how to solve them. Would yet another addition or remodeling be a "greener" solution, more respectful to the site and the environment? Or would their needs be better met in the end by tearing down the house and building a new, energy efficient one?

Describing the Zierdts' quandary, Bryan Anderson remarks, "Increasingly, homeowners are subject to a barrage of products and solutions advertising themselves as 'green' without necessarily having the education or experience to determine the place for these solutions in a broader context. The difficult decision to demolish the house became definitive when we discovered that the attached garage was sitting on a floating slab, rather than a frost footing. This had caused the garage to move separately from the house during freeze-thaw cycles, and it explained the pronounced air infiltration and structural warping between the two." To extensively remodel the entire building envelope, the structure, and the interior is often more costly than new construction. Though demolition results in more material waste, its impact can be lessened by thoughtful reuse of materials. In this case, large, good quality windows from the existing house were reused in the new design. The appliances and flooring were removed by the Reuse Center for future use elsewhere.

The shed roof slopes downwards towards the north, so that there is less wall and more well-insulated roof exposed on that side. Below it, the windows provide views of the Mississippi River.

The first schematic design study revealed that if the house followed the lines of the existing foundation walls, the form that resulted was long in dimension from the north to the south, with its shorter ends exposed to either the river view on the north end, or the sunlight on the south end. People in the house could choose either view or sun, but not both at the same time. Also, the two long sides of the house faced east and west, the most difficult to control for passive solar gain.

The second scheme was a long thin house form, with its long axis placed along the approved setback line from the river. This house form allowed the southern sunlight to reach deep into the house, into the same spaces that enjoyed the north view. Also, the long exposed sides were now facing north and south, the most predictable and thus controllable sides for passive solar gain.

Jeff and Shelly's program specified one-floor living for themselves, plus some additional bedroom space on another level for visiting children or guests. This gave Bryan several opportunities as he explored the form of the house. The main floor space was a good deal larger than the second floor space, which meant the second floor could be on a separate mechanical zone, saving energy when it was not in use. It also opened up possibilities for the form and ceilings of the larger roof over the main level. The form Bryan created simultaneously addressed aesthetic goals, access to light and view, and passive solar strategies. He covered the living space with a simple shed roof. Large windows in a long south-facing clerestory allows southern light to pour deep into the home during the cold months of the year. The home's radiant heat is stored in the mass of the concrete floor. The direct summer sunlight is shaded by a deep overhang on those windows due to the higher angle of the sun during those months. But the light bounces off a flat roof in front of the clerestory windows, lighting the living space indirectly, with less solar gain.

On the north side of the house, the shed roof dips lower to provide less wall and more insulated roof exposure. The windows on the north provide ample, focused views of the Mississippi. A continuous dropped ceiling along the entire length of the northern wall provides an intimate sense of shelter for activities along that wall: dining, a small sitting area for two, and a desk/work space. It offers a contrast to the higher clerestory space over the open living and kitchen areas. It also accommodates mechanical chases and recessed lighting along the length of the home.

The inside of the home is a glowing retreat of light and view. Its walls are crafted almost entirely of warm toned natural hardwoods, 3 1/2-inch shiplapped boards of maple and birch separated by small reveals. The thin horizontal lines of shadow introduce a serene and graceful sense of order within the flowing spaces of the house. The floor is a radiant floor of polished concrete. Its warmth underfoot and subtly colored surface are a perfect combination of function and beauty.

The plan is simple and extraordinarily pleasing. A shared entry for both family and guest use lies under the flat roof below the clerestory windows on the broad south side of the house. It opens to an expansive space containing kitchen and

☙ABOVE: The kitchen work areas are screened by a taller partition of cabinetry, which separates them from immediate view from the living area. RIGHT: The living area is bathed in southern light from the clerestory windows, and enjoys expansive views of the river to the north. A screened porch to the east filters the light on that side. Walls are of maple and birch boards, and the radiant floor is polished concrete.

"I am proud of what we accomplished. I feel like
MY VALUES WERE DEMONSTRATED IN THE PROCESS and result.
No matter where I am in our house, I feel connected to the natural world."

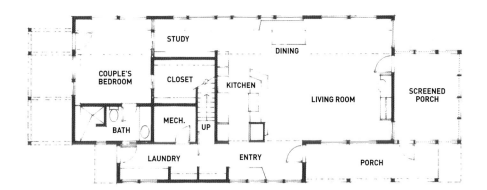

MAIN LEVEL PLAN

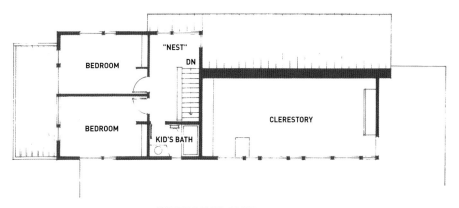

UPPER LEVEL PLAN

LEFT: *A lower ceiling extends along the north wall of the house, offering a sheltered space for the dining area beyond.*

The corridor leading to the bedroom in the foreground doubles as a study, which enjoys views of the river.

living areas, which are open to each other, to the view, to the dining area tucked below the lowered ceiling on the north, and the fireplace on the east wall. Beyond that wall is a screened porch, which deftly filters and controls the eastern sunlight. A trellis on the opposite side of the house does the same for western light.

A study/desk area lined with shelves forms an interlude in the hallway extending towards the main bedroom. Both spaces enjoy river views. A spacious closet and bathroom are adjacent to the bedroom. Because it is accessed from both the bedroom and the family entry, the bathroom serves the needs of both the owners and guests.

The Zierdts' home received a Silver certification rating from Minnesota Greenstar, much to the delight of Jeff and Shelly, Bryan, and the contractor, Showcase Renovation. In the end, they all attributed the overall success of the project to the process by which their many choices were analyzed and selected. Shelly says, "I am proud of what we accomplished. I feel like my values were demonstrated in the process and result. No matter where I am in our house, I feel connected to the natural world."

WELCOMING COMMUNITIES

WILLIAM SARGENT LADD CAME TO THE then tiny town of Portland, Oregon, in 1851. He imported wine and liquor. In 1854 he was elected mayor of the town and began to build a business empire in real estate, transportation, and banking. Ladd was one of the wealthiest and most influential men in Portland in the 1850s. In 1891, he purchased a land claim in foreclosure, 126 acres of farmland in East Portland, from James B. Stephens, who owned and operated Portland's first Willamette River ferry. When the city of Portland was merged with East Portland, Ladd immediately began to plan for the land's future use in anticipation of the light rail transportation envisioned by the city. The resultant community, called Ladd's Addition, is Portland's oldest planned community, and one of the oldest such communities in the western United States.[1]

Ladd planned to subdivide the farm, creating a housing development that would be the most innovative of its kind at the time, including amenities like gas and electric lighting, a sewer system, and paved streets and sidewalks.[2] Having recently traveled to Washington, D.C., he was inspired by Pierre L'Enfant's plan for the capital city. Ladd chose to depart from the prevailing orthogonal grid of the town

1. "Illustrating Four Treatments in Oregon." National Park Service, U.S. Department of the Interior.

2. HAND HISTORY: A brief history by Val Ballestrem (HAND resident and former HAND board member). The Hosford-Abernethy Neighborhood Development website: handpdx.org

FACING: *Ladd's Addition in the Hosford Abernethy neighborhood of Portland, Oregon. William S. Ladd was inspired by Pierre L'Enfant's plan for the city of Washington D.C., and laid out a similarly radial pattern of diagonal streets in his development. The streets revolve around a central green space and four tiny diamond-shaped rose gardens. The diagonal layout defines the feeling of the community as distinct from the surrounding orthogonal grid of streets. When you begin walking along one of the diagonal streets, you know immediately that you are in a special domain. BELOW: Many of the homes in Ladd's Addition address the street with a front porch accessed by a wide, ceremonial set of steps.*

and used an arrangement of intersecting diagonal streets in a wagon wheel pattern. The two major diagonals, which he named Ladd Street and Elliott after himself and his wife, intersect at a circular central park. Proceeding at cardinal points from that center, he established four small triangular-shaped rose gardens. Woven around this configuration were narrower streets, almost all of which were named for various kinds of trees. The residential blocks between those streets were served by mid-block alleys, to screen vehicles and services from view.

Unfortunately, due to a severe economic downturn in Portland in the 1890s, the plans were not immediately put into place, and Ladd died in 1893 before seeing them come to fruition. But his heirs persevered with the development in the early twentieth century: the first home in Ladd's Addition was built in 1903.

Ladd's Addition featured wide sidewalks and planting strips. Garages were located off the alleys behind the homes. Front setbacks of 15 to 20 feet were strictly observed. The lack of curb cuts and driveways in front of the residences created a sense of unity and openness among the front yards. The houses predominately face front, with relatively tall facades, on narrow lots averaging 40 to 50 feet in width and from 5,000 to 6,000 square feet in size. The closely spaced structures stand in rows, like compatible, amiable friends, facing each other across the streets between them. The houses form a community of individual dwellings that are oriented to their neighbors and open to the street and gardens between them. Mature specimens of American elms and Norway maples line the avenues. Their arching branches form a leafy canopy overhead, a sheltering roof for the street.

Almost all of the houses feature prominent front porches. The porches are set back at a uniform distance that is not too far from the sidewalks, creating a sense of shared sociability. Passersby can engage in a moment of friendly chat with those who have emerged from their homes, perhaps to read the newspaper or to water plants. The shared connections from porch to porch, and from porches to the life and sounds of the street, run like invisible threads from dwelling to dwelling, weaving the individual homes and their owners into a community.

Most of the approximately six hundred residences in the development were built between 1919 and 1929. They display an architecturally rich group of early twentieth century housing types, including English cottages, Tudors, Craftsman Style, American Four Squares, Bungalow, Mission Style, and Colonial Revival homes. A majority of the homes include a front porch or a broad, ceremonial front stoop. They range in size from $1^1/_2$ to $2^1/_2$ stories. Built of similar materials used in a variety of ways by creative craftsmen, they feature gabled roofs of medium to steep pitch, broad fascia boards, deep overhanging eaves, and walls of brick, stone, stucco, horizontal wood siding, and wood wall shingles. Because they were constructed in a relatively short time period, they create a deeply harmonious impression of massing, texture, color, and materials. Yet each dwelling is a distinctive individual within the whole.

Ladd's Addition endured a brief period of decline during the 1960s and '70s, when city dwellers became attracted to the promise of life in the suburbs. But it has since been restored and revitalized and is now a thriving community of some 1,669 residents. Its essential characteristics have not changed. It retains the original radial layout plotted by Ladd: small lots of various shapes, an ordered pattern of broad avenues with parking strips, narrower streets, and alleys. The central circular park is used for informal recreation, gatherings and summer bluegrass concerts. The rose gardens are carefully maintained by community members through FLAG, the Friends of Ladd's Addition Gardens. Volunteers regularly meet throughout the growing season, pruning and dead-heading so that the perfumed blooms continue to flourish. Sidewalks retain the original stamped impression of street names, parks, contractors, and construction dates. Original horse tethering rings mark the curbs in front of the residences.

ABOVE LEFT: A cottage in Ladd's Addition. ABOVE RIGHT: A Mission-style home.

The homes, parks, plantings, sidewalks, and streets knit together to form an immensely walkable, human-scale environment, in a district of special historic character.

Ladd's Addition was listed as a historic district on the National Register of Historic places in 1989. More recently, the neighborhood was honored by the American Planning Association as one of the "2009 Great Places in America." As the APA states, "The Great Places program celebrates places of exemplary character, quality, and planning. Places are selected annually and represent the Gold Standard in terms of having a true sense of place, cultural and historic interest, community involvement, and a vision for tomorrow." Portland mayor Sam Adams described it as "a beautiful example of a 20-minute neighborhood, where neighbors can walk or bike to commercial corridors and enjoy parks and open spaces. As the city focuses its attention on climate change and reducing greenhouse gas

RIGHT: *Latavera Cottage, located in the Greenwood Avenue Cottages, designed by Ross Chapin Architects and developed by the Cottage Company.*
FACING: *The comfortable living room is open to the kitchen at the left, and a loft space above. This is a way to make a small area feel spacious and "live large."*

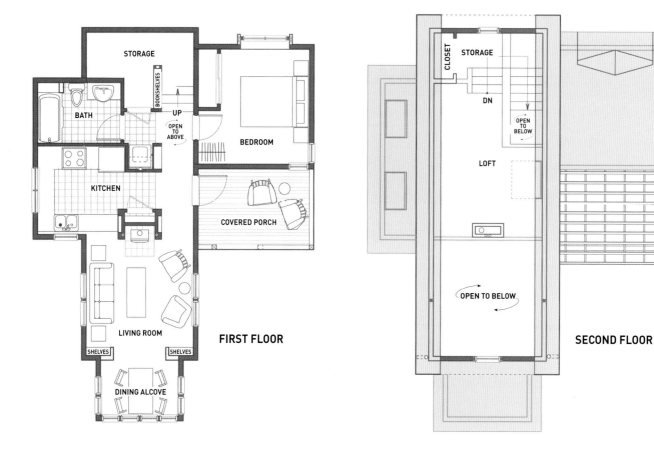

STORAGE

BOOKSHELVES

BATH

UP

OPEN
TO
ABOVE

BEDROOM

KITCHEN

COVERED PORCH

LIVING ROOM

SHELVES   SHELVES

DINING ALCOVE

FIRST FLOOR

CLOSET

STORAGE

DN

OPEN
TO
BELOW

LOFT

OPEN TO BELOW

SECOND FLOOR

emissions by creating walkable communities, it's affirming to see that the origins of Portland's visionary planning and smart growth are embedded in historic neighborhoods such as Ladd's Addition."

In his groundbreaking books *A Pattern Language* and *A Timeless Way of Building*, architect Christopher Alexander examines patterns of recurring events in homes, communities, and neighborhoods. It is these patterns of events that make the places alive. Alexander cites specific relationships of built form and space that are conducive to creating that quality of aliveness. He describes key design components and relationships between them that create cohesive, experientially rich places, at many levels of scale.

His patterns can be used in the design of rooms, houses, public buildings, streets, communities, and neighborhoods. He illustrates the books with photos of natural, unaffected buildings, places, and communities that exude a sense of vitality. The buildings are often regional or vernacular in expression, rather than "high architecture."

As a graduate student of architecture in the mid 1970s, architect Ross Chapin discovered Alexander's as-yet unpublished manuscripts in the archives of the University of California in Berkeley. He was immensely drawn to the concepts described in the writing. Alexander was succinctly describing a method of making architecture that connected it firmly to the physical and spiritual experience of human beings in the environment.

Curiously, Alexander's theories were so contrary to the design theories and methods expounded in architecture schools at that time, that a number of institutions completely forbade their use. (A possible reason for this is Alexander's claim that his timeless method of building eliminated the necessity for both architects and drawings altogether!)

But Alexander's patterns resonated strongly with Chapin's own developing ideas and understanding. He remarks, *"A Pattern Language* gave structure to my felt intuitive sense of things." He studied and assimilated the concepts and then used them as a basis for his graduate work, discretely avoiding mention that he was doing so.

Chapin has now practiced architecture for some thirty years. Since 1982, he and a small group of colleagues have occupied an office in the town of Langley, on Whidbey Island in the Puget Sound near Seattle.

Their work focuses on custom residential design and the development of neighborhoods. The office is a lively place, stuffed with drawings and cardboard

The Latavera living room, looking towards the dining alcove. Designed by Ross Chapin Architects and developed by the Cottage Company.

Each cottage is of a scale that melds with the whole,
but each is an **INDIVIDUAL EXPRESSION.** Each of the cottages has a
name, and they are of varying colors, textures, and details.

models, books, ideas and creative people busy at work. Together with developers, planners, builders, and community members, they produce richly detailed, human scale, environmentally conscious buildings and landscapes that are vibrant and alive. They create places that nurture individuals, families, and neighborhoods.

The firm has become internationally known for its work in developing "pocket neighborhoods." The first such project, called the Third Avenue Cottages, was right in the town of Langley and was a joint effort of innovative and forward-thinking people in state government, banking, development, and the community at large. The city of Langley adopted a "Cottage Housing Development" zoning code. Their stated goals were "to preserve housing diversity, affordability, and character, and to discourage the spread of placeless sprawl."

Third Street Cottages, designed by Chapin and his team, made use of the new code. It is a community of eight small separate cottages that occupy four typical single-family lots, 31,000 square feet in all. Each of the cottages is about 650 square feet, with lofts of about 200 square feet above. The architects' intentions were to provide well-defined personal space and nurture a sense of community. They accomplished this by grouping the eight cottages around a planted commons. The delightfully human scale, 1 1/2-story cottages are nested close together, but each has an "open" side with large windows and a "closed" side with small high windows. The open and closed sides of adjacent houses face each other, so that neighbors enjoy visual privacy from one another.

Parking is located away from the cottages so that each resident passes through the commons each day when leaving or coming home. This encourages the shared daily interactions that are the seeds of community.

Each cottage is of a scale that melds with the whole, but each is an individual expression. Each of the cottages has a name, and they are of varying colors, textures, and details. The shared commons is planted with reeds and shrubs and several twisty-trunk mature trees. A low cedar fence borders the courtyard, punctuated at regular intervals by low swinging gates that lead to the individual cottages. The gates mark the spot that distinguishes public common space from private, individual space. Yet the presence of the courtyard, and the close proximity of the front yards, even the half open and half closed Dutch doors that front the houses, foster neighborly interaction. It is the presence of people and their interactions that bring the community to life. "Living here almost forces you to rethink the traditional idea of being a neighbor and a friend," says resident Brian Ducey. He and his wife sold their 2,300-square-foot house to live in a 986-square-foot cottage in

Cottage gardens and flower-boxes, Third Street Cottages, Langley, Washington.

Greenwood Cottages, another Chapin-designed community. "You really have to become like a family to make it work."[3]

Inside, the cottages are small, but they "live large." Simple volumes filled with light, they feature nooks, eating alcoves, large windows and skylights, and ample built-in storage. Living, dining, kitchen, bath, and bedroom space is all accommodated on the main floor. A ship's ladder accesses a full-height loft space above, with more storage space in the adjacent attic space. They are constructed with simple, authentic materials and details: reclaimed whitewashed spruce paneling, white vinyl windows with white painted trim, and ceilings of plywood and battens. No sheetrock anywhere!

The Third Street Cottages sold quickly, to singles, couples, and small families. The development immediately drew strong interest nationally and received numerous awards for its thoughtful and innovative planning. Chapin and his team received calls from all over the country. Planners, developers, and communities were intrigued by the idea of building less to achieve more cohesive neighborhoods that were energy efficient and consumed less land and resources. It served as a prototypical example for other pocket neighborhood developments, and the design and planning of entire communities within towns and cities.

A number of Chapin-designed pocket neighborhoods throughout Washington share the overall concept of charming cottages of intimate size and scale, clustered around a central courtyard. The role of the front porches on the cottages is key to the success of these socially interactive communities.

Ross grew up in Minnesota, and speaks of his memories of times spent on the front porch of his family's house during those years. The house, on Bald Eagle Lake, was built by his maternal great-grandparents in the 1890s. He describes how life expanded to the porch in the warm times of the year, and how the shared sounds of music and voices drifted from porch to porch along the lake, linking the neighboring families. His experience of "the life of the porch," and how it expressed the world at that time, greatly affected his thinking about what makes shared communities. He describes the ideal porch as an outdoor living room, which "should be large enough to actually be used as a room, and should be placed off an active area of the house. It also should be near the common courtyard, where householders can choose to informally engage with neighbors." Chapin's houses are characterized by some of the most deliciously inviting porches imaginable.

The plantings in gardens in front of the cottage porches vary greatly, according to the proclivities and tastes of the people who live there. A colorful overgrown English cottage garden might be followed by an exuberant garden populated by stones and sculptures, which then might give way to a tiny bubbling fountain

3. Lin, Sara. "The Newest Cottage Industry." *The Wall Street Journal,* July 2008.

The gardens, windowboxes, and furnishings of the porches create
a strong **IMPRESSION OF THE INDIVIDUALS**, yet there is a sense
of contented relationship between the porches and their inhabitants.

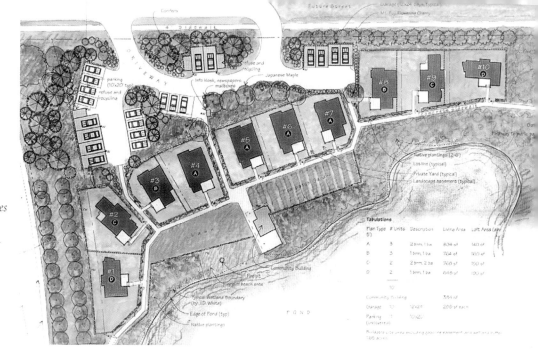

LEFT: *Front porches on cottages in the Umatilla Hill Community. Designed by Ross Chapin Architects and developed by Kimball and Landis.* RIGHT: *Site Plan for the Salish Pond Community near Gresham, Oregon. Designed by Ross Chapin Architects and developed by Michael McKeel.*

amidst the carefully manicured setting of a Japanese garden. The porches themselves are obviously much used, extending the living spaces within the house. They hold comfortable furniture, quilts, pillows, sleeping cats, plants, guitars, books, lamps, and an occasional windsock that shifts in the breeze. Central tables serve many uses: morning coffee, working on a laptop during the afternoon, or a relaxed evening meal carried out from the kitchen nearby. The gardens, window-boxes, and furnishings of the porches create a strong impression of the individuals that live along the courtyard, yet there is an almost familial sense of contented relationship between the porches and their inhabitants. Neighbors greet one another as they leave and arrive, or they chat while tending their gardens. The porch offers a sheltered place to watch the world go by, while still being part of that world.

Another pocket neighborhood by Chapin's group is the Salish Pond community, near Gresham, Oregon, a fifteen-minute drive from downtown Portland. This neighborhood, developed by Michael McKeel, reused and restored land that was previously occupied by an abandoned gravel pit. This development differs in its overall planning approach. Here, the cottages align along a path that extends along the shore of a broad quiet pond. The path expresses a line, rather than a closed loop. The pond is the center of the neighborhood rather than the central courtyard that characterizes many of the other neighborhoods. The cottages engage frontally with views of the path, which links them and the pond in its natural setting beyond. The porches still interact laterally with adjacent porches of neighboring cottages. Like other developments that Chapin has designed, this neighborhood also has a community center building with a porch, which is used for recreation, meetings, and gatherings. Equipped with a kitchen and bath facilities, the building also accommodates occasional overnight guests. At Salish Pond, one end of the meandering shoreline path ends at this community building. Beyond the cottages at the other end of the path is a secure gate, through which residents can access the public walkway that continues around the pond.

The Salish Pond cottage community is unique in that it describes a relationship not only between neighboring structures, but to the landscape, the water, and the wildlife that inhabits that natural environment. The material and colors of the cottages reflect this connection to nature: wood shingles and vertical siding of gray weathered wood. The wood trim is painted in shades of green, gold, brown, and rust. The cottages enjoy a close relationship with their neighbors, but they also enjoy a more introspective distant view to the pond. The interweaving of public and private space is deftly handled; this is a place where even introverted residents could thrive.

Ross Chapin describes his goals as "promoting the richness of human connections. It's not about increasing density but building community, not about frugality, but the *richness* that being smaller and less consumptive of resources can bring about." Over his years in Langley, many of his projects have been woven into the fabric of the town, intrinsically affecting its character. Narrow alleyways have become inviting informal walkways that pass through blocks and connect the streets. The walkways are delightfully planted, and splashed with a pattern of light and shadow by intermittent trellises and vines.

Remodeled storefront facades feature a texturally rich mix of materials and carefully placed ornament. Walking to an outdoor café spot he designed just across the street from the office in Langley, Chapin speaks enthusiastically about the importance of "creating places where people *want to be*. We try to make wholeness at a variety of levels. Houses and communities, when they come alive, are a tapestry of wholeness."

FACING: *The cottages facing east, overlooking the pond.*
BELOW: *Porch and cottage, Salish*

*Pond, designed by Ross Chapin
Architects and developed by
Michael McKeel.*

HOME AND MEMORY

◈ IN THE LATE 1930s MY GRANDMOTHER built a house on a hillside meadow overlooking the Alpine village of Abtenau, Austria. Abtenau is located in a lush green valley, in the Salzkammergut area near Salzburg. The village is surrounded by wooded foothills and majestic mountain peaks on all sides. It consists of a collection of wood and stucco buildings gathered around a central *markplatz* (square), crowned by the spire of a beautiful small medieval church, where my parents were married in 1949.

Throughout my childhood and adult life I often visited this house, which my grandmother ran as a "pension," a small bed and breakfast establishment. Each time I arrived, first as a child with my family, then with my husband-to-be, and later on with our own family, a special note greeted us at the heavy wooden front door. The note was attached to the wide trim around the door, and a sprig of evergreen was placed above it. On stiff, creamy paper, with a narrow black border, the note was written in my grandmother's elegant, rather spidery script. It read *"Herzlich Wilkommen"*: a tender, heartfelt welcome.

A similar message seemed to emanate from the house itself, which was a simple cubic form capped by a deep sheltering roof. The house was simply laid out, divided into four rooms on each level: a kind of Austrian Four Square. All the rooms of the house had substantial shutters, both on the inside and the outside of the house. In the mornings, my grandmother would throw open the paned interior windows, unlock the heavy green wooden exterior shutters, and fold them to either side. The southern light streamed into the kitchen, and revealed a view of her carefully tended gardens below the house, the houses and church down the hill, and the mountain

valley and gray cliffs beyond. We ate our meals at her kitchen table with her guests. The table was nestled into a corner of the room, a "sitzbank" with wood paneled benches built into the walls on two sides. It was a cozy, sheltering, comfortable place that seemed to generate conviviality whenever we gathered there. As a child, I would spend long hours at the kitchen table, gazing out the window and using colored pencils to draw the magical scene outside. My grandmother puttered around the kitchen, cooking the kinds of meals only grandmothers can make. She would natter at me and my mother in German; my mother would answer for both of us. The babbling sounds of their conversations, which I only partially understood, provided a soothing background for my creative (and occasionally mischievous) endeavors.

On the second floor, French doors opened from the bedrooms onto a long common balcony. These were the "primo" rooms, usually occupied by guests of the pension. Thank heavens the guests knew us well. The balcony was a perfect play spot. It was sunny, yet deliciously private and hidden away. When my brothers and I sat on the balcony floor, we were screened from view by the blossoms (usually red) that cascaded from boxes at the balcony railing.

If I had never become an architect, these times would likely have simply been stowed away in a mental file of precious memories. In fact, it was only in the final year of my architectural studies, working on a design for a house, that I was challenged by a teacher to make a place that had meaning to me, one that would "feel good" to me. The exercise was peculiarly wrenching. I realized that in all my previous studies of architectural systems, structure, and theories, I had never yet been asked to seriously consider how one might *feel* as they experienced a place. I had not yet been able to connect the idea of human experience, mine or anyone else's, to the

ABOVE: *My grandmother at the kitchen table in the sitzbank, 1982.* FACING: *My grandmother's house in Abtenau, Austria, 1982.*

creation of places, rather than spaces. Design a place that would *feel good* to me? How the heck would I do that? None of the design tools in my architectural toolbox were adequate for the task. "Architecture" as I knew it wasn't like that . . . was it?

I spent the final year of architecture school immersed in that question. How would I design places that felt good? Places that felt good were in long unexamined memory. For the time being, I tossed aside the question of whether or not they were architecture, as I rediscovered the qualities of places experienced throughout my life that seemed the most delightful, comfortable, engaging, and magical. I became more sensitive to my immediate surroundings and was able to identify characteristics of the places that most satisfied both my body and my spirit. I was beginning to figure out my own personal experiential patterns.

Soon afterward, in 1985, I began working at a newly established local architecture firm called Mulfinger and Susanka. The partners, Dale Mulfinger and Sarah Susanka, were devotees of Christopher Alexander's *A Pattern Language,* and they introduced me to his concepts. The patterns seemed greatly akin to many of my own personal patterns. They just made sense to me. Although I have never designed purely by those concepts, I developed a good deal more confidence and expertise as a designer by utilizing some of them, in combination with those formed by my own life experiences.

The simple comfort and integrity of my grandmother's house, and particularly its strong, reassuring, inviting message of welcome, often inspired my designs. If houses could speak, I think the best of them would say, "Come in. Be safe. Be warm. Be alive . . . Welcome home." As Theresia Mayrhofer, my grandmother, would have put it, "Herzlich Wilkommen."

⌁The barn form is pulled down into the steep hillside. It is composed of a series of related pieces, as if the original form had been added to for years.

Creating such houses is an exercise of the mind and the heart. Both the intellect and intuition play into it. Houses need to keep out the rain. It's terribly helpful to allot the correct amount of space for the microwave, and to place the laundry room in just the right spot. But it is equally important that houses be designed to be nurturing places for our bodies and spirits. To do that, we need to carefully observe and take note of the places and environments, both past and present, where we have felt most at ease, nurtured and alive.

A couple of years ago, I designed a barn-like residence for a couple that had long been enamored with New England barns. Their building site was majestic: a rock cliff overlooking the Pacific Ocean, on the western shore of San Juan Island in Washington State.

Diane Martindale was born and raised in Rockford, Illinois, which is on the Illinois-Wisconsin border. "There were barns galore there," she says, "and each summer we would spend a week or two at my grandmother's farm in northern Minnesota. The memories of those summers—the outhouse, pumping water, feeding the cows, hanging out in the hay loft with kids from neighboring farms—all of it was such great fun! I wanted to know all the different kinds of barns (Wisconsin has them all, including tobacco barns), the reasons for their differences, why they were painted red, and how the silos worked. I would probably have driven my Finnish grandmother crazy, if not for the fact that she spoke almost no English."

Diane also recalls the uplifting feeling of being inside the barns, the almost cathedral-like sense of their structural ribs surrounding an immense yet somehow intimate interior space. She relates, "I particularly enjoyed just sitting by myself in the hay loft. The light filtered through the tiny cracks between the wall boards, making a pattern of light and dark that played though the space, shifting as the light changed during the course of the day."

Years later, Diane and her husband, Steve Bowman, drove through the colorful autumn New England landscape, in search of a particular antique store in Connecticut. On a small road near the Housatonic River, Diane glimpsed a barn near the river. She says, "We pulled over and discovered an old gray barn that had been converted into a home. I was so excited to see that that was possible." The afternoon became a turning point. Her love of barns began to be translated into a dream of building a barnlike house.

In designing the barn house for its steep cliff setting, I integrated it into the rocky hillside by sinking it down into the site, so that one discovers the entry at the heart of a small courtyard space that is literally carved out of the stony earth.

The entire program for the house could have been enclosed in a single long barn form. But to better blend the exterior form with the surrounding landscape, I chopped up the massive barn form into pieces. The exterior shape was interpreted as a series of accreted gabled sheds, casually attached to the main barn, as if they had perhaps been built at different times. Together they create a meandering enclosure around the courtyard. The garage emerges from the hillside at an angle to the house. It is linked to the house by a low-slung building of stone, which is

LEFT: *The dining area is set for a feast produced in Diane's spacious kitchen. It receives afternoon light from the windows facing west over the water.*

LEFT: The stone fireplace in the living room dominates the north wall of the living area. The radiant floor is concrete stained a deep charcoal black. ABOVE: The work area of the kitchen is light and airy, with creamy enameled cabinetry.

capped by a flat green roof. The house is very recognizably a barn at the entry side, but on the ocean side the forms of the house and a deck become more angular and abstract as they proceed down the steep hill. Tapered structural piers of concrete and stone seem to grow out of the rocky cliff and support the deck and house above. They figuratively and literally anchor the building to the site.

Fond as they were of the spatial grandeur of barns, Diane and Steve still wanted the spaces within their home to be comfortable and cozy. Architect Meghan Kell Cornell and I designed the home, with the assistance of architect Maury Stenerson and Judy Ferrell, so that it would feel open and expansive, yet the spaces themselves would feel well articulated and sheltering. We opened up the ocean-facing side of the home with a series of large square awning windows, stacked vertically. The major spaces for everyday living on the main floor are defined by a system of deep structural fir beams. The geometry of the beams and their connections form a framework for the kitchen, dining, and living areas. They are arranged in an L shape that ends at a massive stone fireplace. The slanted form of the fireplace echoes the tapered stone piers outside, which penetrate the interior space of the house. A concrete radiant floor flows throughout the main level. The concrete is stained a deep charcoal black, which contrasts with the bold tones of furnishings and floor coverings selected by Diane and interior designer Bruce Forster of Vancouver, B.C. It also sets off Diane and Steve's extensive collection of artwork by Native American artists of the Pacific Northwest.

The Martindale/Bowman barn house is board on board siding, painted a deep, rich, vibrant red. The silo is of cedar boards, stained with bleaching oil to a light

LEFT AND ABOVE:
Detail of the stair as it proceeds to the lower level. FACING:
The quilting room, with ample work surfaces for layout of fabric.

silvery gray and topped with a domed metal silo roof. Wood and corrugated galvanized steel siding alternate on the ocean side of the house.

The silo form just beyond the entry contains a flowing wood spiral staircase that connects all four levels of the home, culminating in a little round room at the top of the silo, a place for solitary reflection, reading, and observation of the stretch of ocean to the west. The sensuous curves of the staircase railing are outlined with a massive rounded rim that spirals upward and curves inward on itself at the base of the stair. The staircase was masterfully crafted by Dave Kruegar of Lowe Construction. The main bedroom suite hugs the far side of the stairwell; its entry door is a sliding barn door shaped to the radius of the curved wall, which glides along a curved steel track above.

At the opposite end of the house, in the low building form of stone, is a sunny quilting room lined with broad countertops for layout and piecing, and a quilting machine. Diane is an avid and enormously talented quilter; her quilts adorn walls throughout the house. The striking fabric pieces, intensely colored and patterned, provide counterpoint for the simplicity of the surfaces and materials used on the walls and floor.

The upper floor of the house contains three spacious bedroom suites with ensuite baths for the enjoyment of family and guests. Each of the rooms is a work of art in itself, thoughtfully assembled by Diane with an eye to theme, color, pattern, furnishings, and accessories. The "Dick and Jane room," designed by Diane with

Steve's grandchildren in mind, is like a sweet memory of an ideal childhood spot.
It is an absolutely delectable arrangement of colorful fabrics, playthings, painted
furniture, a comfy window seat looking out to the ocean, classic prints of Dick
and Jane with Puff and Spot, books, toys, trundle beds for sleepovers, and a quaint
little activity table ringed with chairs. Diane displays an assortment of antique toys
there, and it is a place for her collection of illustrated children's books. She loves
the gentle stories and the variety of artwork in them.

The other oceanside room, called the "Purple Bedroom," is artfully dressed and
accessorized in shades of violets, greens, and sparkling white. The room is inviting
and lovely; it features a cozy alcove for a daybed below the sloping ceiling next to
the window dormer. It's a perfect spot for an afternoon nap.

Diane's most recent quilt project, fittingly enough, combines her love of barns
and her love of quilting. It is a richly detailed portrayal of the old historic barns
on San Juan Island, rendered in intricate pieces of fabric and embroidery, framed
in a grid of classic red. The quilt, which received the top honor award granted by
the island's quilting society, "seems to have a life of its own," in Diane's words. It
seems that Steve and Diane's long-ago drive through the barn-studded New England landscape has taken root and come full circle in the quilt—and most definitely
in the barn-house they created together.

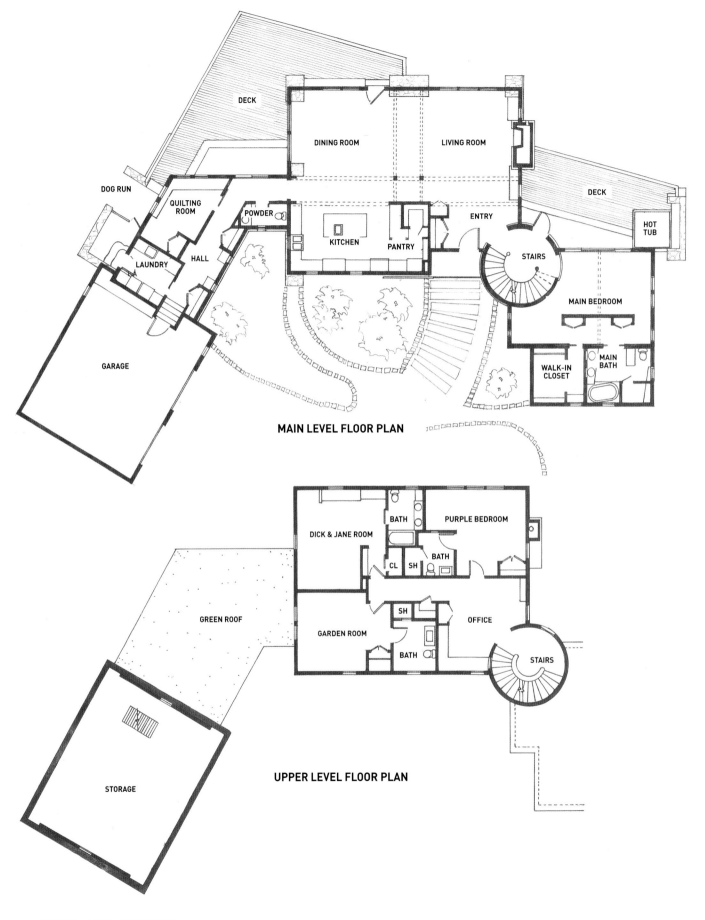

DECK

DINING ROOM

LIVING ROOM

DECK

DOG RUN

QUILTING ROOM

POWDER

ENTRY

HOT TUB

KITCHEN

PANTRY

STAIRS

LAUNDRY

HALL

MAIN BEDROOM

GARAGE

WALK-IN CLOSET

MAIN BATH

MAIN LEVEL FLOOR PLAN

BATH

PURPLE BEDROOM

DICK & JANE ROOM

BATH

CL

SH

GREEN ROOF

SH

OFFICE

GARDEN ROOM

BATH

STAIRS

STORAGE

UPPER LEVEL FLOOR PLAN

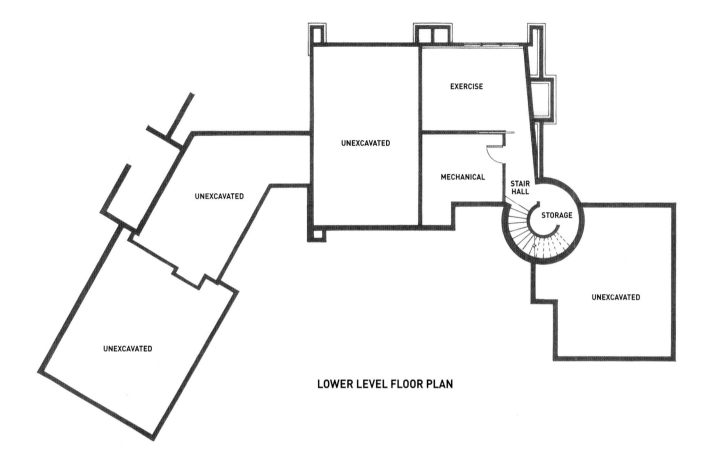

EXERCISE

UNEXCAVATED

UNEXCAVATED

MECHANICAL

STAIR
HALL

STORAGE

UNEXCAVATED

UNEXCAVATED

LOWER LEVEL FLOOR PLAN

Learning to look is a pleasure:
The buildings will embrace your eyes.

Judith Lynch Waldhorn,
from *A Gift To the Street*, 1976

FINDING THE HOME INSIDE YOU

ONE OF THE FIRST STEPS I engage in with clients as an architect is to send them a "programming letter." In the letter, I ask them to describe the kind of living space they envision, whether it is a new house, an addition to a house, or a house remodeling. The programming letter is a document that I have continually crafted and edited over the years. It has become a useful tool to help me understand people, how they live, their values, and how to better design for them. I use it to find just the "right fit" for them, on their land and in their house, just like a tailor might take measurements to ensure the proper relationship of a garment to a body.

The programming letter asks for lots of quantitative information. I ask people to list their needs, their wants, and their budget. (If they are a couple they should do this both separately and together.) Other lists include rooms in the house and exterior rooms on the site. I ask for lists and measurements of furniture, so that we can immediately add it as we begin to create the plans. We need surveys of the property, locations of setbacks, height restrictions, wells, septic fields, water tables, soil borings, and copies of regulations from the state, county, and design review boards that govern building in their area. I ask them to quantify their storage requirements, based on how much "stuff" they have.

I also ask for qualitative information. I suggest that people describe the kinds of spaces they most enjoy, in terms of light, views, and volume. It's helpful to know why they are drawn to a particular piece of land, which of its attributes, physical, historical, or spiritual, speak to them most strongly. I ask about the

LEFT: *A cozy corner dining area in a St. Croix guesthouse designed by architect Katherine Hillbrand, SALA.* ABOVE: *The wood-paneled living area in the St. Croix guesthouse.* PREVIOUS PAGE: *An inviting sun-dappled room in the home of Jo Ann Hammer and John Rupp, on Vashon Island, Washington. The glass-roofed room is a link between the kitchen of the main house and an artist's studio beyond.*

activities that will occur in the home, so that I can shape the spaces of the home to best accommodate those activities. Also useful are lists of materials, colors, textures and finishes that they find appealing, and pictures or sketches of houses and places that they remember from their past or are presently attracted to. One of the most important self-reflective exercises in my programming letter is a journal of how they and their family spend a typical day on a weekend and a day during the work week.

The qualitative information that I ask for is crucial but sometimes harder to get. People seem to be more accustomed to and comfortable with lists of items, facts and numbers, than with describing how spaces feel to them. But both they and I

🔖 BELOW: *An inviting, light-filled room features a built in booth surrounded by double-hung windows. Designed by Paul Buum, SALA.*

☙ FACING, ABOVE LEFT: *A window seat follows the curve of the body and the curve of the window next to it. Designed by architects Dan Wallace and Dale Mulfinger, SALA.* FACING, ABOVE RIGHT: *A comfortable upholstered bench is wrapped into the base of the stairway, in a home designed by architect Meghan Kell Cornell, SALA.* FACING, BELOW: *A sun-dappled window seat in the St. Croix guesthouse, designed by Katherine Hillbrand, SALA.* RIGHT: *A window dormer offers a bright spot to read. Designed by architect Michaela Mahady, SALA.*

need to be aware of the way space feels to them, so that their house can be truly satisfying in the end. I continually try to find ways to help people uncover those perceptions, to find the home inside themselves.

In her recent book, *A Place Like Home,* Toby Israel suggests a series of exercises that will aid people in better understanding the connection between themselves and their surroundings. Israel is an environmental psychologist. Her book is a study of the profound relationship that exists between our past experiences of places and the choices we make now and will make in the future about how we want to live. Her research has led her to conclude that our early experiences, our roots, greatly influence the kinds of places that we are drawn to live in, or as architects, to create. She conducted a series of interviews with three famed architects, Michael Graves, Andres Duany, and Charles Jencks. The interviews revolved around discussions about their perceptions of places that were most significant to them, in their past, the present and the future. Even though each one of them is ideologically dyed in the wool (slightly different wools, of course, from slightly different sheep), their early experiences of place and home seems to have been strongly influential in their work. This was a revelation to all of them.

☙ FACING, ABOVE LEFT: *A charming sleeping room tucked into the volume of the roof. Designed by Katherine Hillbrand, SALA. FACING, ABOVE RIGHT: A sheltering arched alcove surrounds a place to bathe. Designed by architect Michaela Mahady, SALA.*

LEFT: *A unique kitchen is a blend of old and new elements. Designed by architects Michaela Mahady, SALA, and Maury Stenerson. ABOVE: A comfy, quiet window seat in a wood lined study. Designed by architect Michaela Mahady, SALA.*

Israel stated the initial premise of her book, saying, "I believed that each of us possesses our own unique environmental autobiography." She was at that time searching for a new house and decided to explore her own deeply sensed perceptions of home, in hopes that it would inform her search. She guided herself, students, and the architects through a process of environmental self-reflection.

Her research led her to conclude that one's sense of self and sense of the environment are intimately intertwined, and that this connection is rooted in early childhood. She believes that the connection between place and self continues to evolve during the course of our lives, and that we can become aware of the meaning of our deeply held perceptions of ourselves and our environments. This awareness can help us create fulfilling environments in which to dwell. She also recommends that design professionals explore their own place/self perceptions, so that they can better create nurturing places for others.

Following is a series of exercises that examine the feelings created by places experienced in one's past and in the present. Some of the exercises are from classes

and lectures I have given. Others are inspired by the thoughts of Toby Israel, Clare Cooper Marcus, and Christopher Alexander. Understanding the connections between person and place will be an enlightening tool to you, as you go about finding the home inside of you and creating the places you envision in your future. You may wish to keep a notebook of your observations and photographs of places, environments and houses that speak to you.

These reflective exercises will be helpful to you as you begin the process of uncovering, discovering, and creating a place where you can most truly be yourself.

I. LEARN TO REALLY SEE.

Truly seeing the environment around you is a pleasurable exercise of both of the senses and the intellect. Observe your surroundings at home, at work, and at play. Observe and note the way the places feel to you and the way they make you feel. Which are most enjoyable (stimulating)? Which are the most enjoyable (soothing)? Which do you seldom use, and which do you avoid altogether if possible? Are there places you encounter in your daily life that seem uncomfortable, or lonely, or even scary? Why do you think they feel that way?

ABOVE: A built-in bed in a child's room offers a sense of sheltered enclosure, yet it is wondrously open to the world outside. Designed by architect Meghan Kell Cornell, SALA. FACING: Here, the flowing curve of a bench near the entry graciously invites one to pause and rest a bit, while making the transition from outside to inside. Designed by architect Katherine Hillbrand, SALA.

2. EXPLORE AND EXPLAIN.

Note the characteristics of the kinds of environments you are most drawn to. Do you have a favorite spot in your house? What do you do there? Is it a place where you share the company of others or where you are by yourself? What about your favorite places outdoors? Are they closely linked to your house, or are they far away from it? Are they cozy, expansive, or some combination of the two? How do the seasons change your preference for certain places inside and outside your house?

3. ASK YOURSELF QUESTIONS.

Examine your favorite places and your favorite houses. Where have you felt the most nurtured, comfortable and alive? In what kinds of places and spaces do you feel the most free to truly be yourself? Think of all the places you have lived in throughout your lifetime. Record your thoughts and memories about each of these places, in written or visual form. The intent is not necessarily to reproduce those places in built form again, but to discover why they felt so satisfying to you so that you can be aware of the qualitative aspects of places that you innately prefer.

What combination of enclosure or openness, light, temperature, color, and texture comprised those spaces? Are the places defined by walls or separations? Are they covered overhead, or open to space or the sky above? What did you do in those places? Were they places to stand, sit, or lie down? If so, where, on what? What activities happened there? Were there qualities about the place that made it just right for that activity?

4. DESCRIBE THE HOUSE YOU LIVE IN NOW.

How does it feel to drive up to it? Which way do you most prefer to enter it? Is the family everyday entry linked with the one used by visitors? Try to imagine that you are seeing your house for the first time. What does it say to you? What does it say about you?

5. HAVE A CONVERSATION WITH YOUR PRESENT HOUSE.

Tell it how it supports you and comforts you, if it does. Tell it the ways it frees you, or conversely inhibits you. Is it too big, too small, or just right? Does it demand too much from you financially or overwhelm you with its care and maintenance?

Imagine how your house might respond to your thoughts about it.

6. HAVE A CONVERSATION WITH A HOME IN YOUR FUTURE.

Is it in the countryside, in a city or a town, or on the water? Which people in your life is it close to? Is it bigger or smaller than the house you live in now? Describe what you think an ideal relationship might be between yourself, your house, and the land or community around it. Are you separated from neighbors by a wall, twenty feet, or twenty miles? What would that house say to you, and about you?

7. CREATE A COMFORTABLE SPOT.

Make a place in or around your home where you feel completely at ease. It doesn't have to take up a lot of space; in fact, you may find that it is part of a bigger place, defined or carved out from the bigger place so that it fits just you just right. This is a place where you can allow your spirit to roam. Then, devote a bit of time each day to simply being in that spot.

8. FIND HOUSES THAT SPEAK TO YOU.

Consider why you are drawn to them. Look to your memories, to favorite books or magazines, to experiences as you travel. Pay attention as you take walks around your community or drive through the surrounding countryside. Some houses openly beckon; others are more reserved. Which ones would you like to get to know?

9. TRANSLATE YOUR RECORDED IMAGES.

Use your observations to help your efforts when you look for a new home or when you build.

Trust your instincts. Learn to recognize and acknowledge your intuitive responses and understanding. Then take a bit of time quantify these qualitative observations: Carry a small tape measure and camera around with you. Photograph and measure the places that pique your interest or ones that you find exceptionally comfortable and delightful. How is the room or place shaped? Does it have a ceiling? If so, how high is the ceiling? Is it flat, or sloped, or arched? Where is the light coming from? You may find common dimensional, spatial, and proportional relationships in the places you analyze this way. This is an indication that you are uncovering your own personal patterns.

10. PUT THE PIECES TOGETHER.

Weave them together with an eye to incorporating the personal spatial patterns that you have discovered.

a. Study the relationship of the house to the sun and the views on the site. Are the view and the sunlight on the same side of the house or on different sides? Which rooms need the view, the sun or both? Are there spaces or rooms that need little or no view or light, or where light from above or borrowed light from an adjacent space might be more pleasing than through a window in a wall?

b. Think about the relationship of rooms to one another inside the house. How are those places connected or separated? Where will people sit, converse, read, gaze at the fire or watch television, cook, eat, work and sleep? How many places do you need to do each of those activities? Can some spaces serve more than one activity at different times of the day or the year?

c. Think about the kind of shape the house has, inside and outside. How does the roof form cover the places and rooms in the house? What does the house form say to you? What does it say to the land or community around it?

11. DISCOVER THE PATTERNS IN THE HOUSES THAT SPEAK TO YOU.

Find out when they were built, who built them, and for whom they were built. If they were the result of a purposeful design process, seek out the work of that architect or designer and see what you can glean from it. Sometimes people have the skills necessary to translate their thoughts into built form themselves. But if you find yourself at a loss in this translation, find architects or design professionals whose work speaks to you and who will listen to you. They can help you create a house that will comfort you, nurture you, and welcome you home every day.

ABOVE LEFT: *A pleasing shingled house in Sand Creek. Designed by architect Paul Buum, SALA.*

BELOW LEFT: *A timbered log house on a sturdy stone base. Designed by architect Katherine Hillbrand, SALA.*

ACKNOWLEDGMENTS

A BOOK, LIKE A HOUSE, is the product of many hands and minds. I would like to express heartfelt thanks to the people who have helped to create this one.

Thank you so much to the homeowners who graciously permitted me to photograph and write about their homes: Jim and Karen Nancekivell, Eric Odor and Cory Barton, Wayne Branum and Ann Routier, David and Linda Hickman, Mark and Barbara Youngdahl, David and Theresa Deming, Mark and Bonnie Matuseski, Mark and Therese Mahady, Rick and Linda Glasgow, Jeff and Heather Swanson, Brad Bruno and Toni Schaeffer, Jeff and Shelly Zierdt, Diane Martindale and Steve Bowman.

Thank you to all the builders and craftspeople whose talents, knowledge, and energy brought these homes into existence. Your work will live long to shelter and delight future generations.

Great thanks to Gibbs Smith for inviting me down the path of writing a book, Dale Mulfinger, who encouraged me along the way, and Lisa Anderson, my editor, who patiently and wisely guided my words and whims throughout the journey.

Warm thanks, too, to Peg Quinn for her help in reviewing the initial draft; to Rick Commandich and Maya Muir, who introduced me to Ladd's Addition in their beautiful city of Portland; Margo Nielson, for showing me the children's house drawings in the HIP housing calendars; architect Katherine Hillbrand for words of wisdom; Diane Dahl for acquainting me with the work of the Life Science Foundation and the University of Minnesota Center for Spirituality and Healing; and to architect Robert Gerloff, whose thoughts inspired my programming letter.

In particular, I feel great gratitude to my partners and colleagues at SALA Architects, both past and present. They are treasured friends and teachers. I am so very fortunate to be a daily part of the creative and caring community of SALA.

And enormous thanks to my best friend and husband, John Pietras, for his enduring support, insight, and wisdom. I am especially grateful to John for the consistent clarity of his eagle eye, ever vigilantly spotting yet another overly lengthy sentence.

RESOURCES

❧ HOME PLANS

www.architecturalhouseplans.com
Maple Forest House, 2006 Cottage
Living Idea House, September Cottage
(Swanson home), and Carriage House/
Studio

www.notsobighouse.com/plans/index
1999 Life Dream House (Back to
Basics) and 1999 Life Dream House
(Whole Nine Yards)

www.rosschapin.com
Latavera Cottage, designed by Ross
Chapin Architects

ARCHITECTS

SALA Architects, Inc.
www.SALAarc.com
info@salaarc.com
Minneapolis Office
  326 E. Hennepin Ave., Suite 200
  Minneapolis, MN 55414
  612.379.3037
  fax 612.379.0001
Stillwater Office
  904 S. 4th Street
  Stillwater, MN 55082

651.351.0961
fax 651.351.7327

Ross Chapin Architects
www.rosschapin.com
inquiry@rosschapin.com
PO Box 230
Langley, WA 98260
360.221.2373
fax 360.221.8603

Bentley Tibbs, AIA, Architect
www.bentleytibbsarchitect.com
tibbsaia@sbcglobal.com
3711 Parry Ave., Suite 203
Dallas, TX 75226
214.676.6478

Rehkamp Larson Architects, Inc.
www.rehkamplarson.com
info@rehkamplarson.com
2732 W. 43rd Street
Minneapolis, MN 55410
612.285.7275
fax 612.285.7274

BIBLIOGRAPHY

Alexander, Christopher, Sara Ishikawa, and Murray Silverstein. *A Pattern Language.* New York: Oxford University Press, 1977.

Alexander, Christopher. *The Timeless Way of Building.* New York: Oxford University Press, 1979.

Bloomer, Kent C. and Charles W. Moore. *Body, Memory, and Architecture.* New Haven, CT: Yale University Press, 1977.

de Botton, Alain. *The Architecture of Happiness.* New York: Pantheon Books, 2006.

Bugge, Gunnar, and Christian Norberg Schultz. *Stav og Laft (Early Wooden Architecture in Norway).* Oslo, 1969.

Chiras, Dan. *The Solar House: Passive Heating and Cooling.* White River Junction, VT: Chelsea Green, 2002.

Day, Christopher. *Places of the Soul: Architecture and Environmental Design as a Healing Art.* London: Thorsons, 1999.

Hale, Jonathan. *The Old Way of Seeing: How Architecture Lost Its Magic (And How to Get It Back).* New York, 1994.

Israel, Toby. *Some Place Like Home: Using Design Psychology to Create Ideal Places.* West Sussex, England: Wiley-Academy, 2003.

Jung, C. G. *Memories, Dreams, and Reflections.* Rev. ed. New York: Vintage, 1989.

———. *Word and Image.* Princeton, NJ: Princeton University Press, 1979.

Kahn, Lloyd. *Shelter.* Bolinas, CA: Shelter, 1973.

———. *Home Work: Handbuilt Shelter.* Bolinas, CA: Shelter, 2004.

Marcus, Clare Cooper. *House as a Mirror of Self: Exploring the Deeper Meaning of Home.* Second ed. Lake Worth, FL: Nicolas-Hayes, 2006.

McAlester, Virginia, and Lee McAlester. *A Field Guide to American Houses.* New York: Knopf, 1984.

Moore, Charles, Gerald Allen, and Donlyn Lyndon. *The Place of Houses.* Berkeley, CA: University of California Press, 1974.

Mulfinger, Dale. *The Architecture of Edwin Lundie.* St. Paul, MN: Minnesota Historical Society Press, 1995.

Norberg-Schultz, Christian. *The Concept of Dwelling: On the Way to Figurative Architecture.* New York: Rizzoli, 1985.

Norman, Donald A. *Emotional Design: Why We Love (or Hate) Everyday Things.* New York: Basic Books, 2004.

Rasmussen, Steen Eiler. *Experiencing Architecture.* Cambridge, MA: MIT Press, 1959.

Rapoport, Amos. *House Form and Culture.* Englewood Cliffs, NJ: Prentice Hall, 1969.

Scully, Vincent J., Jr. *The Shingle Style and the Stick Style.* New Haven, CT: Yale University Press, 1971.

Susanka, Sarah, with Kira Obolensky. *The Not So Big House: A Blueprint for the Way We Really Live.* Newton, CT: Taunton Press, 1998.

Wedlick, Dennis. *The Good Home.* New York: HBI, 2001.

PHOTOGRAPHY AND ILLUSTRATION CREDITS

BRYAN ANDERSON
Page 177

WAYNE BRANUM
Page 85 (bottom)

PAUL BUUM
Page 220 (top)

ROBBIE CAPONETTO
Pages 58–75

ROSS CHAPIN
Pages 184 (plan illustrations), 184–185 (photos), 186

PAUL CROSBY
Pages 9, 40–49, 221, 223

CHARLES DAVIS SMITH
Pages 93, 96

DAVID FERGUSON
Pages 56–57 (plan illustrations)

NICK GORSKI
Pages 117, 120 (top), 122–133, 213, 214 (top right and bottom), 215, 224

SARAH GRESHOWAK
Pages 66 (illustrations), 67 (plan illustrations), 89 (plan illustrations)

ART GRICE
Pages 7, 195, 199–207

KEN GUTMAKER
Pages 22 (bottom), 23

GEORGE HEINRICH
Pages 3–4, 6, 12, 15, 52–57, 81, 85 (center), 86–91

COURTESY OF IOWA STATE UNIVERSITY
Page 119

CHRISTY JOHNSON
Pages 38–39 (plan illustrations)

DEBRA KEES
Pages 160–161 (plan illustrations)

MEGHAN KELL CORNELL
Page 110 (plan illustrations)

CHRIS KOCH
Page 85 (top)

BALTHAZAR KORAB LTD.
Page 104

PETER LEE
Page 84

GLENN ROBERT LYM
www.lymarch.com
Pages 82–83

MICHAELA MAHADY
Pages 16, 17, 21 (illustration), 60 (illustration), 100 (illustration), 103 (center and bottom), 118 (illustration, after sources noted), 146, 209

KAREN MELVIN
Pages 108–115

MORGAN MOSIMAN
Page 18

PHILLIP MUELLER
Pages 24–37, 38–39 (photos)

DALE MULFINGER
Pages 120 (bottom), 121

GREG PAGE
Pages 154–161

COREY PEDERSON
Pages 50 (plan illustration), 168–169 (plan illustrations), 206–207 (plan illustrations)

JOHN PIETRAS
Pages 11, 94–95, 99, 134, 145, 148–153, 178–179, 181, 188–194, 196–197

YANA PIETRAS
Page 14 (illustration)

COURTESY THE CITY OF PORTLAND, OREGON
Page 180

CHABRIELLE SCHUTZ
Pages 5, 101, 105–107, 135–141, 163–169, 210, 212 (bottom), 214 (above left), 217, 220 (bottom)

ADITI SHARMA
Page 22 (illustration, top)

TROY THIES
Pages 76–79, 103 (top), 162, 170–177, 211, 212 (top right), 216, 222

DAN WALLACE
Page 212 (top left)

JESSICA WILDER
Pages 132–133 (plan illustrations), 138 (site plan illustration), 152 (plan illustration)

PETRONELLA YTSMA
Page 144